Don't Get It Twisted !

Poetry & Short Stories

P.O.P Writers Guild

Brenda L. Stovall • Adrienne Bruce • Linda Gaddis
Katerria "Starr" Doty • JoAnn Wesley Hassler
Lenita McCullor • Kelly Clark • Ken Allison

authorHOUSE®

T0196761

AuthorHouse™
1663 Liberty Drive
Bloomington, IN 47403
www.authorhouse.com
Phone: 1-800-839-8640

Published by AuthorHouse 6/28/2013

ISBN: 978-1-4817-7107-8 (sc)
ISBN: 978-1-4817-7106-1 (hc)
ISBN: 978-1-4817-7105-4 (e)

Library of Congress Control Number: 2013911455

This book is printed on acid-free paper.

Cover & Graphic Art: Valerie Winkfield
Typesetting & Editor: Brenda L. Stovall
Biography Photos: Michael Whittaker
                        Adrienne Bruce
                        Brenda L. Stovall

Forward

Pen on Paper (P.O.P) was created for the purpose of gathering groups of individuals who are like-minded and who have a passion to express themselves through a variety of writing styles. P.O.P was also formed to birth new ideas and stimulates gifted writers to push out their thoughts and share their inner feelings with potential readers through a plethora of publications.

"Don't Get It Twisted" is the first born of volumes to come from this group introducing both neophytes and sophomore authors including founder, Adrienne Bruce, along with Brenda L. Stovall both who have published works and introducing Linda Gaddis, JoAnn Wesley Hassler, Katerria "Starr" Doty, LeNita McCullor, Kelly Clark, with Ken Allison and graphic artist, Valerie Winkfield who have collectively come together to produce this body of work including poetry and short stories for your enjoyment. Sit back, relax, and "Don't get it twisted!"

Love,
Adrienne Bruce
Brenda L. Stovall

Index

Don't Get It Twisted

I used to know that man
By: JoAnn Wesley Hassler

I used to know that man
I thought
As I took my seat at the baptism/naming for my
youngest grandson
Our grandson

He looks old, needs a haircut
Dressed a little too formally,
The woman next to him was vaguely familiar;
I met her once.

I used to know that man
I thought
As I took my seat at the baptism/naming of my
grandson
Our grandson

How does one greet a man she has known
(In the biblical sense)
For over forty years?
It is awkward; he looks old
Do I?

I used to know that man
I thought
As I took my seat at the baptism/naming of my
grandson
Our grandson

Do you erase all that has been?
Do you boast how good life is now?
That it is no longer shared?
Do you start a conversation?
(Or wait for one)
To evolve

I used to know that man
I thought
As I took my seat at the baptism/naming of my
grandson
Our grandson

Unable to resist,
I approach,
Ask silly questions
About the house
(We once shared)

I used to know that man
I thought
As I took my seat at the baptism/naming of my
grandson
Our grandson

Strange, little to say,
We have gone our own way
A few comments about the day,
Work and play

He is ready to retire
(And I am) going strong...
His new woman approaches, marking her territory...

I used to know that man
I thought
As I took my seat at the baptism/naming of my
grandson
Our grandson

I realize I let go years before
The awkwardness passed
He is hers with my blessing
A blessing neither wants nor needs.
I have given more years, energy and thought to
This sunken ship...

I used to know that man
I thought
As I took my seat at the baptism/naming of my
grandson
Our grandson

I needed to see them together
At a family affair,
See him as grandfather and father
With his new life intact
To truly let go
Of what I no longer wanted

I used to know...that man!!!

Don't Get It Twisted
By: Kelly Clark

I'm about to put my twist
On this
Question
So you will not
Miss
Out
On what I'm trying to say
About the things happening today

So hold on still
And listen up
Keep an open mind
And don't interrupt
Until I complete
My full conjecture
Then I will give you
Time to lecture

And here's my twist on this....

You Got it Twisted

By: Brenda L. Stovall

My twist on this is
That you got it twisted
You already missed it
A long time ago

Because if you
Would have listened
To my directives
You would be on
The righteous road

But you rather
Go left
Than go
Straight
You rather not love
But instead hate

You rather fail
Than graduate
You rather jet
Than marry your mate

You rather sling
Than have a job
You rather steal
Kill and even rob

You rather have diamonds
On your teeth
Than on my
Finger

You rather have gold
In your mouth
Than a marriage
To remember

It's not even
A May December
Romance
It's just a timber

And fall
We have no land
More money on rims
No helping hand

You want respect
From me
And you not even
A man

Twisted Sister
No Mister
No house built
Just sinking sand

Normal

By: Ken Allison

I long to be normal
Doing things normal people do
Being vulnerable, laughing, crying, showing affection
things
I used to do......

Long before my life changed
The days when decisions weren't so intense
Doing things for no specific reason
Things that didn't always make sense

I miss saying I'm sorry simply when things didn't go our
way
Not because some life threating things my actions
caused
Was headed our way
I long for normal days

I remember normal nights holding each other
Simply because we were in love with each other
And it was alight.

If I could do this life all over again
Fantastic would have no place
I'd live a life
Doing normal things
And that would be okay

My Spin on This
By: Lenita McCullor

It's a sunny day
And my dreads are blowing from right to left
Because of the fan that's in my face.
This intriguing pen and paper
Is sitting on the table and one thing came to mind.
Poetry it's therapeutic to my soul,
It touches every atom and molecule
On the inside of me,
Oh Poetry it heals the brokenhearted,
It eases the pain, it dries up the tears
From weeping in the midnight hour,
Oh Poetry just like when the birds are chirping
And the waters are moving and the trees are whistling
And the wind is blowing,
Oh Poetry it feels so good to hear you
It feels so good to read you
It's wonderful to see you because you are a delight
Oh Poetry how you caress me
How your words come alive on the inside of me.
It heals me mentally, encourage me spiritually
And ease me physically
Oh Poetry! Oh YES, that good Poetry!
That good speaking reading poetry
It's therapeutic to my soul.

Pieces of My Soul
By: Katerria "Starr" Doty

He's doing us both,
It's time we make a stand,
For we are a woman's worth
After all I said and all you know
I think it's time to let that man go
One thing I hate is
I lowered my standards
And borrowed what you have

Actually I didn't gain anything,
Instead lost pieces of my soul
Now I must repent to God and hope
He lets it go,
Or else there will be another
Love TKO
I've learned one thing
Married men are married men
They don't mean you no good,
Unless you'd like to be
Damned for good

WHAT DO YOU WEAR TO A RIOT?
(Observations of the 2012 - NATO Summit held in Chicago)
By
Linda D. Gaddis

What do you wear to a riot?
Hadn't you thought about that?
When NATO came to Chicago
Should you have worn black?
Should you have dressed up?
And came downtown
Wearing your finest
Silk or satin gown

The gents not to be outdone,
Could've kicked it up a notch or two
By wearing a fancy tux
In lilac, peach or powder blue
To top it off, let's give them a hat
That's both stylish and a bit crazy.
One that's trimmed with a tiny fur band,
Displaying a rather large daisy

By all means try to avoid
The casual shirt and tie
'Cause that would mean
You represent that 1% guy.
Those corporate few protestors
Plan to state

That is the reason our country
Is in financial straits!
Dress as a protestor,
Come in plaid shirt, white shirt, t-shirt,
No shirt and jeans.
Carry a placard displaying a slogan,
Making a point, just don't be obscene.
You could wear a 'hoodie'.
Oh, wait I guess not!
Why run the risk...
Of being shot?

Show up as a concerned homeowner
With janitorial garb on
So you can assist in the clean up
Once protestors are gone

Come as an anarchist
That's right fully clothed
Totally black with bandana and hood
(If you choose to be so bold).

However, cover your face
And talk really loud,
So you can appear
To blend in with the crowd

Maybe show up as nurses
Dressed in uniforms of white
When the protest is staged
At the Daley Center site

Go one step further...
A 'Robin Hood' costume
To demonstrate the robbing the poor
By the rich, I presume

If you're truly committed
You could plan ahead
Consider the colors wheat or brown
And come as a loaf of bread.
Walk along side
An oversized can of SPAM
To protest some agriculturally wrong
While listening to Willie Nelson,
Bob Marley or Will-I-Am!

Come dressed as an opposing nation
Wearing your country's flag
Be sure to cover your face
With a large brown paper bag
And express your disgust
And mistrust of the U.S.
About their unauthorized involvement
In the international mess

Military dress is quite proper
And will most certainly be allowed
When you start tossing those scared medals
To demonstrate your objection to the war, now

Join right in with Speedo's
While coming in on a bike
So you can contest fossil fuel
And some other environmental plight

Why not prepare yourself
To be an international host
So you can travel the city with the 'First Lady'
When she starts to boast
About the south side Comer Center
To the other spouses in the NATO group
Then continue with a Limo excursion
And dinner at the Art Institute

How about an outfit
Of a chef highly skilled
As you serve up sumptuous dinner fare
For NATO dignitaries down at Soldier's Field

Better yet, try dawning
Some official clergy attire
And super charge the NAC of Defense
With a speech filled with "brim stone and fire".

What if you went as a resident of South Loop?
University Village or neighboring areas around
Take care of all business a few days
Before the Summit,
Then pack your bags, canine and kids and leave town.

Why not dress as a chauffer
Wearing a suit of jade
And bring the dignitaries from the airports
To the Loop, as part of a motorcade

Suit up as a lawyer and wear a cap of green
Bring 'biz' cards with services you provide
Just in case things get out of hand
And you have to cover a protesters hide.

Dress as a nun in a black and white habit
This way you can show your support
Besides who is going to take
An activist Nun to court?

And what do you say?
How'd police dress that day?
As they get NATO bound
They don't mess around.
Uniform design, simply great!
Included everything except Batman's cape

Imagine Chicago PD all geared up
With over 8,000 additional face shields for its cops!
Each one is said to fit
Over gas mask equip.
This they feel will help to fend
Any liquid and stuff protesters might send.

It seems for all the fuss
That some individuals made
And the high level of attention
That the media paid
-
More chaos and confusion
Had been planned
Some figured the CPD
Would be out manned

But thanks to quick thinking
 Community concern and police intervention
It was the summit not the city
That was the center of attention

So in the end it didn't matter what you wore
People really didn't give a hoot
If you or someone else
Showed up in their birthday suit!

Just in case, for some reason,
You missed an opportunity to participate
I'm sure you'll get another chance to dress
In the year 2028

Never Offend a Vendor
By: Adrienne Bruce

This is an actual correspondence between an event promoter and a vendor attempting to do business together. It is deep needed to share it.

Sent On Feb 16, 2012 10:53 AM,
To Adrienne---- From Nicole

Hello,
I saw your creations! They are unique and beautiful works of art. I understand their value and worth. However, my honest opinion is that the guests most likely expect to spend a little less for their jewelry per piece than what yours are. I feel it's my responsibility to tell you this beforehand verses you spend the money on a 50 or 85 dollar booth and not do well. I don't just take money from vendors, I actually want them to profit because I sincerely care. If you have product that's say maximum fifteen- eighteen dollars for earrings then, ok. But if not may not work. And I dare not ask you to comprise your jewelry value.
I wish you much success!!

Sent: Friday, February 17, 2012 8:10 AM

To Nicole---- From Adrienne
Thanks Nicole for that advice, I have studied the buying patterns of our people. I am going to be honest

and think about what I am about to say. Blacks will spend lots of money for Coach, Burberry, Dolce & Cabana, Prada, Gucci, Baby Phat, Air Jordan's, and many other designers and fatten their pockets. Majority of these people are not African American. I have quality one of a kind pieces. We need to get out of that Korean and Dollar Store mentally. We have to stand together and educate our people. We will go to Water Tower and spend $100 for designer jeans or 65.00 for our favorite perfume. Why can't we spend with each other? If you are in an elegant environment and fine dining then why not have a quality product. I have product starting a 25.00. You can't get my product in your local department store. So if you will stand with me to educate our people I will attend. Blacks buy what they want. Stop selling them short or cheap.

Just Being Real
BBless
>Thanks
Sent: Friday, February 17, 2012 11:22 AM
To Adrienne---- From Nicole

Adrienne,
I appreciate your honest reply. I always welcome a platform for non-hostile, open discussion. Therefore, I thank you in advance for our friendly exchange. Now please, allow me to also, 'be real'.
I, like you am a black woman well versed, educated and articulate. I stopped patronizing Korean hair supply houses 6 years ago upon going natural after I, as Marcus Garvey said, 'Took the kinks out of my brain

and not my hair.' I was ridiculed from our people from a personal and professional standpoint, being begged to,' Please let me perm your hair so it can be pretty'. Ha! How lost of a people we are that we have bought into Euro ideology of what beauty is, even if it means accepting that our God-given features aren't already beautiful! To this day, older aunts will ask from time to time when I will perm and after years of my friendly, 'let's love ourselves' rant they continue to be mentally trapped, so now I just smile when 'taunted'.

I have never asked my parents nor as an adult purchased Air Jordans, Gucci, Mecca, Prada, Baby Phat, Louis, Coogi, Burberry clothing or perfumes. My parents were married, hard working individuals who promoted the RIGHT priorities. My brother and I studied music, took up two instruments and frequented the Ravina for operas and symphonies. Why we met YoYo Ma and Ramsey Louis and B.B King! We developed a love for jazz, classical and blues music and weren't allowed to listen to rap. Art and history museums of all cultures were visited and my mother made us write tiny reports on them- outside our homework! We went to the beach, flew kites and had peaceful picnics by the lake.

I tell you this because I consider myself a very OPEN minded person. I was raised to enjoy and pursue interests that other black kids were taught to think were boring. I was teased for being articulate as a child, when really the kids and their parents were and I hate to say, close-minded ghetto folks who didn't try to expand and learn new things to better their lives. All they knew was fried chicken, fast food, Kool-Aid and soda, rap or R&B, baby mamas and daddies, Ghetto

Urban Wear, expensive cars and things when they couldn't even afford their utilities! I agree that Black people need to refocus. We need to visit art museums and explore our past. We need to stop damaging our communities and making them crime and drug zones. It only sets us back. We need to treat our bodies better, eat well and exercise so we no longer become the poster children for heart disease, diabetes, stokes and hypertension. We need to be educated on how to invest in stock market, IRAs and ownership instead of committing financial suicide focusing on 'bling-bling' or non-essential purchases that depreciate and are valueless. When I ride down Madison I just hurt from how our people have gotten lost. So PLEASE, PLEASE understand me that I understand YOU! The people attending (the ones I know personally, can't vouch for all) are kind, will give a needy person their last and are very respectful. However, I would admit that most of us are closed-minded, that's why for example, I keep my natural rants to myself cause blacks can be stubborn, unwilling to step outside the box and try something new. Maybe some of us are too cool, I guess. We blindly follow trend but won't be original. And gosh, we treat each other with such disrespect, not cool! I called myself sparing you a financial loss in the event the kind but closed-minded attendees pass you by without patronizing your business. I try to treat people like I would like to and that's why I was honest cause to be it wasn't about just getting your money. I hope you understand that element of it. Yes, it drives me nuts how our people can be. And heck, they may surprise me...Maybe it'll encourage our people to visit the art museums. I'll share my guest membership passes! Anything for the cause.

So in conclusion, if you are ok with taking a possible risk...I dare not stand in your way. I already commended you on your talent and am sincere about that.

Just tell me how you'd like to participate!! I'd love to have you. Our guests need diversity, yes-teach them! Perhaps I gave up too soon...will admit error.
Nicole

Sent: Friday, February 17, 2012 1:26 PM
To Nicole---- From Adrienne

Thanks for your honesty! Wow you had a lot inside begging to get out. I advise you to Blog about it. This just may open up some of those closed minds. Do you mind if I share this Email? And I too grew up like you. Thanks and keep daring to be different.
Yes I will proceed! I can't wait to meet you.
BBlessed Today!

Adrienne Bruce
Beautiful Blessings

Sent: Friday, February 19, 2012 12:19 PM
To Adrienne---- From Nicole
Hello,
Are you still interested in joining us for the expo Friday 3/23 and need an extension pass today's

deadline? Let us know...we will be glad to have you!
Nicole Taylor

Sorry, I was so winded but I promise you that my
husband and I talk about this all the time so your
response struck a chord, lol.

I do love our people; there are tons of good things I
cherish. And I love soul food and prefer dusties from
Herb Kent, so I'm 'down' too, lol!!! We just need to be
more accepting, open minded and supportive.
I'm done, you may share it. Hope I'm not villanized
cause that was just you and being frank. I didn't mean
to offend anyone.
Let me know soon and purchase your table, people are
calling me a lot lately.
Such a pleasure you are!
See you soon.
Nicole

On Feb 19, 2012 1:30 PM
to Nicole ---- From Adrienne
No need to be sorry I needed to here that and others
need to hear it to'
Thanks for sharing
BBlessed
I will purchase my table on Wed.

Music

"I hear music in the air!"

Negro Spirituals

Adrienne Bruce

Singing Old Negro Spirituals
Makes me proud to be
African American

While listening to
Old Negro Spirituals
I stand up tall and stick out my chest
Knowing I'm favored and blessed
To be a part of this heritage

I can hear the struggle in the hum
I feel the pain my ancestors sung
I see the path they journeyed
I visualize the dance of freedom

Listening to sweet melodies
I join in and feel a connected presents
The soft beat of the African drum
Moves and stirs my inner soul
I close my eyes and I'm there
In the past slowly moving toward now

Singing Old Negro Spirituals
Makes me proud to be
African American

I Love Music
Brenda L. Stovall

I love music
Any type of music
With the pizzazz
Of jazz
The rhythmic sounds
Of Brass

The sounds of the
Sax, Son!
From Babyface
To Tone Tony Toni
Braxton

And the careers of
"This is no ordinary love"
What a way to spend the day
Sippin' wine eating cheese &
Stepping to Sade

And you know I just can't
Forget about Patti
Nor Gladys, or Chaka
And they not even catty

From Nina Simone
Michelle Ferrelle
To Jill Scott
And Patti LaBelle

Hey Marvin
What's going on
So Why don't we get together
After the Dance
I don't see nothing wrong

Because I rather live
With him in his world
You're all I need to get by
The reasons that we're here
Because I need you to survive

Mariah puts your soul on fire
You getting in the way of what I'm feeling
You better call Tyrone
To pick up your bag lady

And you better slow down
Too tie up your Loose Ends
As I ride the "EL"
Because we're just friends

I know you were formerly Prince
King of Pop I'm told
Mary J. The queen
And James, The Godfather of Soul

Because like Minnie
I'm loving you
James would you woo, woo, woo
Luther won't you wooooooooooo me too

Music
By: Lenita McCullor

Holding back the years, hoping this music can last till the end of time. Gradually tiptoeing trying to follow the sound! This sound is different; all races are moving to this beat. They are Jamming and they are smooth with their feet. Pushing and pumping clapping and stomping!

Wow... Now that's music, no voices just the guitar and the tambourine thumbing. Now what sound do you hear? When I scream what pitch of my voice will make you move. This music that I hear will give you more than just the blues. The sounds are high with no never ending end, and the beats are outrageous could this be an epidemic because this can't be contagious

This sound brings me back to a place of no return and one day this will be the place, where a community beast will arise, awakened spirits and shaken streets. This music that I hear is cries of mother trying to survive and a father doing his best and never had a paternal guide. Could this be an epidemic because this can't be contagious?

I'm trying to rowel this lion and let them know I got them faded, hear me when I speak, develop yourselves and stop trying to compete. You're original and there are none like you. You're skillful and gifted. And I know because it's in your spirit.

Since music is the device in getting your point across, let's have some new pushing and pumping, clapping and stomping. Wow! Now this music can change lives on any day and give hope in many ways.

MY THOUGHTS ON MUSIC
By
Linda D. Gaddis

I've got nothing to say about music.
I can talk on end
About the latest trend
But, I've got nothing to say about music.

I've got nothing to say about music
I can moan and groan
About being monotone
But, I've got nothing to say about music.

I've got nothing to say about music.
Some of it's totally absurd.
Look at Dizzy, Coltrane and Byrd.
They all had great styles
Let's not forget Basie and Miles
When we talk about the music I know not.

I've got nothing to say about music.
Someone mentioned a guy named Jimi,
He paid musical tribute to many.
The "Star Spangled Banner" he played,
Setting his guitar a blaze
Gee, I wish I knew something about music.
I've got nothing to say about music.

Dinah and Billy were the ladies around.
Chandler and Ellington were the Dukes in town.
The Temps and James were the Kings.
Aretha and the Supremes were Queens.
Music's history I try to grasp but cannot.

I've got nothing to say about music.
Heaven knows how hard I've
Tried and I've tried,
To understand syncopated beats
And count notes with both feet.
Still I've not time to play this music thing out.

I've got nothing to say about music.
If with instruments we begin
Let us start with the winds,
Then move on to the strings
And wind up with percussion and things.
 My, I wish I knew something 'bout music.

I've got nothing to say about music.
I've tried many a time
To place rhythm with rhyme
Play chords on a keyboard.
Use a guitar to strum along.
Test my vocals with a song.
There's reason no more
To be a musical bore.
I must now stop and go
Learn me something 'bout music.

What I Do, I Respect it!
Ken Alison

The one thing I do
And respect whole heartedly
And enjoy
Is music
Whether I'm writing a lyric,
Composing the melody,
Arranging a song
Or merely relaxing and listening
To music I respect the art
Music has always been an important part
Of my life
As it is the sound track
Of my life,
The joys, the pains, the heartaches
Or the victories can be
And are mirrored in the music
Of a particular song
Or a particular artist
Version of a song
Why I respect music
Is deeper than the fact,
That music is universal,
It reaches, it touches everyone,
It has been said that
Music soothes the savage beast
I can't help
But to respect
Music and above all else
I love music

My Pandora's Box

JoAnn Wesley Hassler

My mother loved Broadway Show Tunes
I knew every word by age 12
She never sang but shared and savored
The theater experience
On 33 1/3 vinyl long playing albums
No opera at our house...
Just songs with a story
She hummed

I sang as a teen
Pat Boone, Johnny Mathis, Connie Francis...
Slow dance party songs,
Never a good dancer but an
Assertive singer who knew the lyrics,
 I preferred folk song sing-a-longs...
John Denver, Peter Paul and Mary...
And rather than show tunes, music from the movies.

Young Mom..."Kiddy Songs"...Lullabies,
Sesame Street, Mr. Rogers
Easily sung with a less than perfect voice to an
Appreciative, interactive audience of three toddlers
In three and one half years who later joined me
In serenading their little sister

Inspirational music and relaxing spa music
To sooth the overworked soul
In my less than peaceful home filled with
And then emptied of teens leaving
For college, a busy career that paid their tuition
And Music quieted the sadness in letting go.

36

Then there was the
"I am Woman Hear Me Roar"
Of a woman coming into her own
Aided by the lyrics and voices of
Bette Midler, Barbra Streisand,
Whitney Houston, Tina Turner, Cher,
Dolly Pardon, Tony Tennille...
Hanging on, keeping on, moving on...
It's what women do.

Music bears the gift of transporting to a time and place
Filled with memories of treasured faces, places and moments
They say when one can no longer speak, they can sing
I have a Pandora's Box waiting for such a day!

Music
By: Kelly Clark

Boom, boom, boom, boom
I feel the music, I live the music
Boom, boom, boom, boom
I hear it every day.
Boom, boom, boom, boom
I feel the music. I love the music
Boom, boom, boom, boom
It tells me what to say

Don't hate me! Don't judge me!
For playing what I feel inside.
Debate me berate me
When what's moral and what's real collide.
Cause I'm only trying to share
What I see and what I know
And in time you're going to see
That I told you so
But until then, just listen to my melody.
It will do you better
Than any other therapy

It will relax you. It will excite you.
It will take you high. It will bring you low.
It will soothe you. It will move you.
It will teach you things. It will make you grow.

WIDE BOTTOM

By: Katerria "Starr" Doty

He's slender wide bottom
I caress and hold him close
I thrumb his pain with my finger
As he lingers near ...me

I captivate him, I'm smooth
Like him, slender thighs
That's so easily walk by yeah
He feels me...hears me...he's on top of me

You see he's slender wide bottom
I caress and hold him close
 I thrumb his pain with my finger
I play sweet melodies as you let me dig deep...

Because you complete me, let's be intertwined
Rhythms of love, concentrate on you
I'll play for you
Because you're more than just a sweet valentine

U see I'll oblige while your fingers ride waves of strings
And create sweet melodies, sings like no 1's business
Not to mention, I'd play your troubles away
And help to create a brighter day
You'd pay to hear my work of art
My fingers would caress and hold you,
I'd try not to let it go
I thrumb your pain with my finger, as he lingers
near.....me

I'd play sweet melodies
My fingers would bring you nearer
As I'd pour sounds similar
To a symphony inside you serenading you

I'd pick those strings so softly
And finger the slender neck
And wide bottom of that lead guitar
To get those everlasting sounds and effects,
Music sweet music
I'd neva abuse it

Unemployment
"I Need A Job Bad!"

UNEMPLOYMENT WOES

Linda D. Gaddis

It seems that everywhere
      One goes
There is talk of
      Unemployment woes
It's hard these days
      To find a job,
And without one
      You're called a slob.
Without a job
      You won't get
A nanogram
      Of self-respect
Now everything
      Is so darn high
Gas prices rocketing
      To the sky
And the price of
      Milk and cheese
Will surely bring you
      To your knees
Oh Lord,
      Can it be?
There is absolutely
      No hope for me?
No money, no house,
      No food, no job,

Oh God, why are times
    So hard?
Tell me please
    What I must do
So my condition
    Will soon improve?
I figure if I
    Keep the faith
Things will go from
    Bad to great!
If I can just hold on
    And just wait...
        How long...?

Hold On
By: Lenita McCullor

What do you do?
When you're in a place you never been, the wind has
blown in your direction and now you're feeling erections,
but not of pleasure, pain of contractions has filtered
itself everywhere because of this burden that has come
upon you. While trying to relax your emotions, tears
begin to flow because of what you feared the most.

What can you do?
Being unemployed for too long and you could complain
because sometimes it feels good, but my problem is still
there, and who cares. Right! I'm tired of been broke
and please stop telling me Lullabies and water down
clichés. Yes I believe GOD, but my condition is in my
face. I feel like a river with no water, just empty. Now
I'm on my bending knees begging Father please help me
or take me. See sometimes trials and tribulations will
make you feel like you don't want to be here. I know you
saved, buts let's still keep it real.

What should I do?
You should encourage yourself. Faith without works is
dead, so apply your faith to his plan, "for I know the
plans I have for you, plans to prosper you and not harm
you and give you an expected end". Allow God to order
your steps and eventually you will get ahead, stay
faithful and obey and keep his commands. Not what you

want but what his word says and remembers he will
never leave you or forsake you. See his
promises and covenants are forever just follow
Almighty God's unchangeable hand. He is not a man and
he cannot lie and his word will never return back to him
void, so continue holding on and just hold on because in
a little while you will hear his voice.

Unemployed?
By: JoAnn Wesley Hassler

If you are not making money...
Are you unemployed?
It is the question the self employed
Grapples with each
And every day

When punching a clock, reporting to a desk daily,
It is clear there will be
A check at the end of the week;
Payment for services rendered.

For the self-employed entrepreneur
The same activities accomplished...
At the end of the week...a paycheck?
If not...is she unemployed?

Can she fire herself and
File for unemployment?
Does she qualify for Food Stamps?
Section 8?

Not counted in the figure
Released by government agencies
The one that count those working and those not
Does she count at all?

Does anyone know the struggle?
Or how close what she does is gambling?
Waiting for the nest windfall, big order...

Compensation...
Feast or famine
Roller-coaster of highs and lows
Creating debt and catching up
Eternal optimist...

Is there such a thing as debtor's prison?
Does she qualify? A roof over her head
And three meals a day...Some days it
Doesn't sound so bad

Why do this?

To create a life of her own making
To have time to be with family, friends
To live her values have time to play,
Travel, write, create
Unemployed...no...never...
Employed in the business of living a life
Punctuated by work

Work that weaves
in a meaningful way
The fabric of a maverick
Who is willing to risk...?
To Be the "Different Drummer"

No Safety net other than the one
She creates for herself in knowing
She had the definitive partner...
A loving God who is her
Ultimate resource and significant other

Unemployment
By: Kelly Clark

Unemployment- lost my job!
It's too many of us, were like the mob.
Sending out resumes everywhere we can
Getting no responses! How much can we stand?

The gas is getting cut off today
The repossessors are on the way
Baby needs a new pair of shoes
And we got a light bill due.

It feels like I'm going insane
I got too much on my brain
How I'm going to pay that
How I'm going to keep this
How long will I exist.

Unemployment-lost my job
It's been to long I'm becoming a slob
Staying in bed not wanting to bathe
Depressed and ashamed no longer unscathed

Don't know if we can ever return
Don't know if we'll ever get it back
Once confident and sure independent and secure
Now living with fear, poverty and lack

Unemployment- lost my job
It's too many of us were like the mob
Sending out resumes everywhere we can
Getting no response how much can we stand?

February 3, 2009
By: Brenda L. Stovall

February 3, 2009
A day my paycheck went blind
Head on collision accident
To Loyola Hospital is where I went

My pastor didn't let the congregation know
No get well cards, no compassion shown
Injured to surgery I have to go
Snap-On laid me off 5 days before the show

Heartless cold on disability
3 surgeries in one year
Dear old me
It's either food stamps or SNAP
But can't receive no check
How can I make too much money?
I'm just a reject!

Can't find no job
"Well are you looking?"
What a stupid tale question
Makes me feel like crooking

But I'm not a crooked person
But HE made my paths straight
Stimulus from Obama
My mortgage still awaits

Still in my house
Cause of the Lord
It's because of HIM
My windows aren't boarded

Lost a lot of friends
Over a period of time
Money buys you love
Phoniness is such a crime

Waiting on Medicare
To kick in
Part A, B, & D
For my medicine

But above all
God is a healer
Unlike the world
Who is a stealer!

Keep to myself
I have no true friends
When your rich you're the (ya know)
But God he's till the end

Without him
I don't know where I would be
Or how I survived
This long journey

3 years I've been broke
Congress cuts
Our unemployment checks
And Cobra is just a joke

Just like that snake
Bank of America
BOA is your true name
I wish my name was Erykah

So I can get a window seat
And go on vacation
And truly find
A Holy Nation

Thank God for Jesus
Because I wouldn't have made it
He kept my lights on
With him I have credit

Price Paid in Full
Just because of his love
I may mean nothing to you
But I'm worth more above

So people hold your head up high
Unto the Father lift your voice and cry
Yes my Father in Heaven can hear
I pray for you it will be a better year

Don't give up or give in
Because the Lord will be your friend

September 24, 2003

By: Katerria "Starr" Doty

Never would have thought
Wow how could this be?
Me.....
A house to be, on the line
A whole lot now racing through my mind
Fired me?
At 2:33
September 24, 2003 at 2:33

What will I do?
I couldn't see clear so I focused
Looking him in the eye,
But in my mind I was saying goodbye

Goodbye to co-workers, customers
And mostly bye to working outdoors
Walking in all seasons
Sometimes enjoying the breeze
And trees

Kids talking to me,
Watching animals in their natural habitat
Honestly I felt like balling,
I was afraid of the unknown
I had to be strong through it all
As I searched the vineyard for my timecard
People stared at me as I
Walked to the postmaster's domain

I remained strong
Even though things just went way wrong
My mind was so clouded,
I was in disbelief
I now needed peace
I had no choice but to stand
I'm free to be me

I walked out the post office door
Never to revisit anymore
I don't want to bore you with my troubles
But I was in a bubble
I felt like now it's time for me to be a rebel
Unemployed, I was fired from the Post office
At 2:33
Who me?

Now where will I go making $50,000 at 25?
With no college degree
Oh wee, I'm nervous
How will I provide for me?
And my family, my baby and me

I gotta dig deep, deep inside of me,
Yeah me what's my
Destiny
What can I birth within me?
And be beneficial to those depending on me

Unemployed
Can you say annoyed
We don't have to be unemployed
Dig deep inside of you

What's on the tip of the iceberg of your mind?
Get on you grind, restore your mind,
Hindsight I smite, punching a clock from 9-5
I'm alive and captain of my own ship
Set sail...bail unemployment

Employment
By: Ken Alison

I thank my parent
For instilling in me and my six siblings
A work ethic that defines us all
I am fifty eight years old
And have worked literally all my life
As a young child household chores
Were my first responsibility

We all had our duties and they were determined that
we
Would need no-one we would be able to fend for
ourselves
Boys washed dishes, did laundry, learned to cook etc.
Girls took out garbage, shoveled snow, mowed the lawn
in Addition to doing the more traditional girl-boy duties
My parents reasoning were we would not need husbands
or Wives to complete us.

By the age of nine I was self-employed in addition to
lawn service, snow removal. I also sold X-mas cards,
delivered groceries as well as hustled pop bottles by
the age of ten I worked with my father whose services
included moving and hauling, plumbing, tree surgeon
among other things and to this day my home service
company still provides these services and my ten year
old son is my apprentice

Employment is a staple in my life and I am proud to have been and presently employed with the City of Chicago for 36 years as of July 26 which has earned my social security benefits from previous jobs.

My job that I love the most is being a performing artist and I have been a member of local entertainment community for forty three years professionally.
So you see I believe and am proud to say employment is a blessing that keeps on giving.

SHOES

Adrienne Bruce

Seems like only yesterday I was wearing a shirt and tie
My life was good and I was on a natural high
Making a six figure salary, money to burn
Traveling the world was easy never a concern

Now look at me sitting here on the ground
Jobless and hungry and no food around
Watching whispering people pass me by
Have no more tears even if I wanted to cry.

Hey! You over there whispering about me?
Take a walk in my shoes you will surly see
How I came to be

Hey man!
Here, take my shoes put them on
I want you to see how my life went wrong
Can you feel the rocks beneath my soles?
These shoes have a story! So much to unfold...

Can you see the mistakes?
I've made from which
I have not recovered!
Do you see the people?
I've hurt and disappointed
Including my father
And loving mother

Keep walking there is more
Look at the house
That burned down
Due to my smoking
The job I lost
Because I got caught stealing.
Look at the women I've abused and used
From one side of town to the other
Right there is the jail cell
I slept in many years
Because of the street fights,
Gambling and too many beers

Hey don't take my shoes off,
There is more tragedy that followed me
Look at the five children I abandoned
Three pretty girls and two handsome boys
Wanting my attention
Just stupid!
How could I avoid
The most precious people in my life
My children and I had a wife
Where are they now?
Where could they be?
If only I could see them not them see me

Keep walking
Can you to see?
The painful path
I journeyed

Look up!
There's the dark cloud
That hovered over my head
Twenty-four seven
This clouds was trying
To keep me from Heaven

These are the same shoes
That were free to roam
Showing me a good time
Keeping me away from home
These shoes did get tired
Of pacing the sidewalks
Going nowhere fast
I often wondered how long
This life style would last

Sitting here on the ground with my shoes off
Don't want to go any further my life is so screwed up
Always hearing "In God we Trust...God will make a way!"
God please make a way today
Before I give up and pass away

If you took off your shoes
And gave them to me
Would I be surprised?
At what I might see
Next time you laugh
And giggle about me
I hope you're ready
To release your life story

Gone Too Soon
"I want to go there..."

DISCO ANGEL
Linda D. Gaddis

My heart is heavy.
    Her spirit light
Seems another angel
    Has taken flight
In Naples, Florida,
    At the age of 63
LaDonna Adrian Gaines,
    This world did leave
You may not know her
    By this name
Say 'Donna Summers'
    Then you'll recall her fame
"Lady of Disco",
    "Disco Queen"
She dominated
    Every disco scene
Starting out in church,
    At the age of ten,
Her musical talent
    Did begin
Her neighborhood
    Had her back,
They'd offer her funds
    When she was "strapped"

They had a feeling
    That she would be,
Some very,
    Notable celebrity
About their money
    No fuss was made
When she became famous
    They knew they'd get paid
And famous,
    She did become,
With 19 charted hits
    That became number one!
Beyonce paid tribute
    When she wrote,
"Her music made me move..."
    Was her partial quote
President Obama
    Did concede
She was truly
    "The Disco Queen"!
Although the battle to lung cancer
    She did not win
Ms. Summers was a fighter
    'Til the very end
She shall be missed dearly
    By family and friends

37 & Beautiful
Adrienne Bruce

She was 37 & Beautiful
A caramel complexion
Long silky hair
Living a life
Others wouldn't dare
Married, two children
You would think
Her life was fulfilling
Good job opportunities
Always thrown her way
But never seemed to be
Happy day after day
Loving parents raised
Their one and only child
To live life to the fullest
With her beautiful smile
Running away from home
The streets she did roam
Her mind played tricks
Causing her body
To yearn for a fix
The darkness of night
Swallowed up her life
She was 37 & Beautiful

I Don't Love You
JoAnn Wesley Hassler

So many reasons for divorce...
Disrespect, Dishonesty, Disconnect....
But it never occurred to me to say, *"I don't love you."*
I wanted to leave, live alone, be free...
I did not realize the real reason behind the divorce was
I did not love him any more
When does love stop?
How many times in how many ways
Did I think?
I could resurrect something that
Was gone...dead...finished.
"I don't love you"
Simple
It was the reason to stop trying, stop lying, let go...
Four little words
The demise of a once strong, confident love
"I don't love you"
The door is closed

Ode to Trayvon
By: Brenda L. Stovall

I can't feel
The rainbow
But I feel
The pain though

Of this bullet
In my back
Eating skittles
As I get whacked

Some say it's race
Because I'm black
Neighborhood watch
Has attacked

Because my neighbor
Says I'm suspicious
Why has this world
Grown so vicious

I'm drinking Arizona
Then I get popped
Hand in my waistband
Where are the cops

This Man is walking free
My blood lay on the ground
I would be locked up
If this was the other way round

Like Cain and Abel
Are you my brother's keeper
Instead of watching the block
You've become the Grim Reaper

You suppose to call 911
And hang up the receiver
I pray for your soul
Are you a believer

So Father I commence
My soul to you
For these men don't
Know what they do

We can make test tube babies
Put man on the moon
But how do we prevent
Another Black youth leaving here
Too soon

Gone to soon
By: Lenita McCullor

My life changed on January 1, 2007. That's a day I wouldn't ever want to relive. I woke up that morning so excited for another New Year. We made it as the church folks would say. The phone is still ringing and the ringtone is singing happy New Year.

I kept rubbing my stomach because I had a seed that was soon to come. Scratching and holding my back, thinking how I'm gone plan this year and Father please help me, because you know how I am.

Man what a New Year, hours later my New Year turned into new fears and new tears because of the devastating news I received, my baby brother gone, it just can't be, he was not too long ago here with me, laughing and joking talking about our younger days.

Life goes on, that was Challah's song. My feelings were all over the place and I had to be strong for my parent's sake, at least I thought. My soul was mourning and I wanted to retaliate. His life was taken so Young.

I can't even begin to tell you what was going on inside of me. Looking at him lay in that bed, no breath in his body. Apart of me didn't accept he was gone. I'm yelling Challah let's go home. Please let's go home.

My little brother I miss him so! 21 years you were here with me and even though you're gone ever seems like the best Year to me. Leaving me has taught me how to love in spite of and how to celebrate people while their still here.

I appreciate you and I know you're smiling from above. Mom and Dad are doing better and because of your life, we've all learned how to love. Your gone but never forgotten until I see you again, I will continue to live on and remain strong.

Music Therapy
By: Kelly Clark

There you are! You're on top!
Everyone's calling your name.
You got the best of things.
In the best of places
While many bask in your fame

But, as fate would have it
Fame takes a stronghold (as it often does)
Then the test and the stress of the World
That once loves you, starts to unfold.

Now you can't cope you feel empty inside
You can't tell truth from a lie
You become dependent on any kind of suppressant
To hide the pain you can't deny.

Fame is tricky and highly deceitful
It pretends to be your friend.
It gives you lots of money and lots of things
That gets left behind in the end.

Along with the lovers and haters of you
Your siblings, parents and seeds
Everyone's grabbing for what they can get.
After the spirit inside you concedes.

To Anyone Who's Ever Lost A Loved One
By: Ken Alison

We had no idea you were leaving
On the morning that you left
By his grace and tender mercy
He called your name
As you slept away into the heavens
To take your place at his side
Leaving us heartbroken
We cried

We wept we sighed without a clue
No suffering no illness
That we knew only God knew
The plan when he sent
His angels for you

In his mansion there are many rooms
Filled with serenity and peace,
Leave all your trouble and sleep
He knew that we would miss you
And all the sorrow there would be but
He also knew we'd figure it out
Acceptance is the key so farewell my daughter,
Sister, brother, son, aunt, uncle and dear friend
This is a new beginning for our memories
Of you will never end

Miss You Grand Daddy!
By: Katerria "Starr" Doty

I miss you Grand Daddy!
I recall many things about you
I always had beautiful Easter baskets
Money cards, and always greeted with a smile
I think back to days of looking at pictures
Of everyone on that coffee table
I still hear your laugh,

I'm smiling because I just heard you again in my mind
Memories, sweet memories
I'm reliving thoughts of you from our past
Oh here's 1,
Remember when I purchased my first car from your
wife
The Hyundai excel
Remember the brakes went out,
You wanted to give me my money back

Or when I was a mail carrier
And we began dating each other
We had tons of fun,
You always insisted on Old Country Buffet
I ate so fast
BBQ sauce soiled my white shirt,
We ended at the laundry mat cleaning that shirt
I should have known then something wasn't quite right
You snapped on Kenya
And wouldn't let me outta sight

I Miss u Grand Daddy!
Yeah the time I trailed you
On the toll way
Going to my place
You drove 30 miles an hour the entire way,
While people flew by honking and giving us the bird
I'll never forget the call
Saying you'd been in a terrible accident

I remember cleaning your face from blood and debris,
Those stitches you had to get
I remember when Alzheimer's came
And barged through your door
I still laughed with you as you played
The funky chicken on your tape recorder
You danced and made those chicken sounds,

As you played it again and again
Although I laughed and smiled with you
I knew you would never be the same
We had so much unfinished business,
I bought our fishing license together we went on 31st
street
We still had so much unfinished business
I've walked in your shadow in so many ways I am a true
Doty

I've delivered the mail, bar tended,
And began my own business
Just as you did
I'll never forget the day
You came to my apartment

And told me you were proud of me
You said to continue on the right track,
So I will try my best to keep doing my thing
Cause you last saw me as your best

Money
"The Burdens We Must Carry"

MONEY MATTERS
Linda D. Gaddis

It's just money
    So they say.
But try to do without it
    For just one day.
You might get by
    Two weeks, maybe
After a month even homeless
    Look at you crazy.
What now makes you
    So much better
When you don't have
    Postage for a letter
Once a penny
    You had found,
You would leave it
    On the ground
Now if one is
    Within sight,
You stop whatever,
    And take flight.
To get that
    Shiny copper piece
If you find enough
    Then you can feast.

At any select
>Food venue
Where you can dine from
>The dollar menu
Remember when only
>Macy's would do,
When it came to
>Shopping for you?
Now if Target
>Has your size
It's cost, not cloth
>That catches your eyes.
Money may not mean
>That much to you,
But if it I don't
>Get some soon,
I don't know
>What I'll do!

Ode to the self employed
By: JoAnn Wesley Hassler

No more 9-5,
That is
Girlfriend,
The lure of entrepreneurship

Long Hours, Weekends at Work
Cash flow problems,
No paid vacations
Do it yourself health care.

CEO, COO, CFO...
You wear every hat.
How well does each one fit?
Is it worth it?

What does it take?
An iron will,
Attitude
A sense of adventure
An ego the size of Manhattan

It is the American way
Capitalism
At its best
Earn what you are worth,

You choose
Not to have a boss,
But be the boss
Is it worth the risk?

For this woman,
With an independent spirit
And a love of freedom
It is the perfect fit.

Is life really all about the Benjamin's?
By: Adrienne Bruce

Every time I look around somebody got their hand in my
pocket. And they just won't stop it, Time to pay this,
time to pay that by the time I get a paycheck my money
is whack
Fireman and Police calling me on the phone
Donate to what, Hey man that's wrong
I already pay city taxes that's not enough
Hey it's rough ~ out here
Folks always wanting me to pull my money out
I know some things got to be paid no doubt
I ain't got it like that, they just don't understand
My money is gone before it gets in my hand
I already have bills that go on for days, months and
annual dues

Most of the time I feel I've been taken and often times
used
The mortgage or rent I don't know which one you pay
As long as you live this bill never really seems to go
away
Don't forget the light, gas and water bill
Got to have these if you want to live ~ comfortably that
is
Please don't get sick that will cost you too
You will even get sicker when the bill gets to you
This bill is in the thousands you just look at it and laugh
You have got to be kidding, a funeral is less
But I want to live so I got to pay this mess

If you have any money left after all of these
Let's not forget the groceries
Got to eat and want to play
You know entertainment cost a lot today

Wither you go to the movies, a play or concert
When you get the bill you feeling will be hurt
Got to have gas in my car if I want to drive
And gasoline is always on the rise
God knows we can't walk around without clothes
Got to have the latest if you want to be choose
Those designer jeans and stiletto, Oh so hot
I put them on my credit card they cost a lot.
Let's not forget my make-up and hair
Got to have it done before I go anywhere
The question was: Is life really all about the
Benjamin's?
Are the Benjamin's running your life.
Causing you strife
It seems I can't go from day to day
Without having something to pay~for
What about you?

Mutha Lovin' Cash
By: Katerria "Starr" Doty

Fresh outta the shower
Lotioning my Ashe,
But on my mind I need some
Mutha lovin' cash
The kid's dad produces no ends,
So it's up to me to bring the flow
Of revenue in
I gotta make this cash,
It's just me,
Just me, myself, and I,
If I don't get this green
Is not gonna just come to me
Money to pay these bills,
Plus we wanna live
And keep a nice house
And some material things
The jeep yeah,
We wanna reap the benefits
Me and the kids
On the up and up
I'm gonna show them this world
We will explore
Not only outta our backdoor.
We won't just hear stories being told
I'm ma b bold
We gonna explore these countries,
Why because it's our liberty
On my mind I need

Mutha lovin' cash
To build a teen home
For pregnant teens
Without families
To help them build young
Their self- esteem, etiquette,
And knowledge to raise themselves
To standards way above this society,
And their children to be more than
Wanna bees.
Money I use it to buy
And make it when I sell,
Money is what for some feel no pain,
Others...just too dam vain
Money has been known to be
The downfall of many
And brought joy to some the same
Money gone in this here millennium
Has taken many for broke,
Some have even said
"Just give me a rope!"
Depending on your intent
Moneys good to bless
Those in need
And get some desires
Of 1's heart
Money can't buy happiness
But confusion totally!
Be supreme
Put trust with God
No money
And we will have the desires of our hearts

Money

By: Kelly Clark

Gotta go to work
Gots to get paid
Gotta get my hustle on
Don't want to live afraid.

Gotta punch that clock
For over 8 hours
Gotta hit the block
To feel the power

Of making money
For myself
Stacking paper and
Acquiring wealth

For my family
And my posterity
To heal the city
And community

America

By: Brenda L. Stovall

Some people live for it
Other people die
Other people steal it
Other people lie

Some will cheat on their taxes
Some on their spouses
Some even break into
Other people's houses

Some will take abuse
Some will gain fame
Others are willing
To defile their name

Some will bury their dead
Others dig up graves
Others search on their phones
Looking under their "Favorite Favs"

Some step on toes
Some lay in bed
Some sell blows
Others give head

Some "slip and fall"
Others take risks
Some go DePaul
And others Fisk

Some indulge
Others embezzle
Others make music
And that's "4 rizzle"

They say America is
The Land of Milk & Honey
But they will do anything
To make that money

Money
By: Ken Alison

Money, Money, Money, Money-Honey
Honey, Honey, Honey, Honey-Money
My baby drives me crazy
And I love her to death
But her craving for materials things is greater than our
Money and that leads to debt.
How like any man my woman's happiness is priceless
But like most women
Her appreciation is far less
What I did yesterday was cool and nice
But it's as though even
The thought depreciated in value over night

Money, Money, Money, Money-Honey
Honey, Honey, Honey, Honey-Money
My baby builds me
When were alone
Doorbell rings a whole other spirit enters our home
Her baby did this her man bought her that
Baby when you gonna take me there, don't you even care
I have love that's deep, and runs true but sometimes baby I
Feel I can't afford you
Sometimes I want to say I love you, but there only words
What's the value of that, money can't buy you love
Or is that still fact,

Money, Money, Money, Money-Honey
Honey, Honey, Honey, Honey-Money
AINT GOT NO MONEY

Money

By: Lenita McCullor

Your existence was here with me since I can remember.
I'm sweating uncontrollable because now I'm nothing
without it and I will do anything to keep it. As I drift
off gazing in the mirror, holding you up on a pedal stool
as my king, cause you know I done things like that.

You will always multiply my barnyards as I would call
them. You constantly filling me and feeding me. You
continue to pump me with lies and I'm smiling saying yea
I like, this alright. How much more can I have of you.
Man I need this and I'm gone do anything to get it.
That's right anything to get it.

I'm sitting at the dinner table, pissed off as hell, I
couldn't tell time and time couldn't tell. See you
magnetic to me, your value cause seductive ways in me
to illuminate and then I'm ready for penetration in such
a way.

Your craftiness has me delusional all the time and now
I'm addicted. My left eye is twitching because now I'm
thinking on how to get out this place, who's hurting I
am. As fast as it comes that's how quit it goes. I have
allowed these guys to rule me and take control.

Benjamin your currency has paid mortgages, exotic fun
and trips for. Grant and Jackson you done big things on
many days, you kept my car laid and the kid's tuition
paid.

Lincoln and Hamilton the gas has never been shut off, lights are still on and water is still flowing. Oh, I can't forget about Washington and Jefferson thanks for the low days and the little tools and fuels you gave.

I heard the love of money is the root of all evil and that it can be a blessing or a curse. Now I know my Father in Heaven is the real provider for me and He will always come first.

"Proud of my beauty"
Freestyle

Room of Her Own

By: JoAnn Wesley Hassler

As a young girl in a family of eight

I longed for a room of my own

Never did I suspect it would take so many years

To accomplish the dream

To satisfy the craving for time alone

An extrovert in an introvert's body

I longed for solace, quiet, space...

A place for reflection and creative expression

I longed for a place where the Muse

Could beckon, tease and taunt

A space where my frazzled spirit

Would come to rest in a web of words

That expressed the deep longing

To weave a tapestry that would capture

The Essence of my soul...

(NOT SO FONDLY)
THINKING OF YOU
By
Linda D. Gaddis

It causes me pain
      When I think that you
Saw nothing wrong
      With the things you'd do
And say the awful things
      You felt the need to say
To try your best
      To make me stay
         (With you)

You have gone
      To extreme lengths
To destroy my character
      And wear down my defense.
And so that I
      Would never stray,
You'd demean me
      In every way

You called me names,
      That's not okay!
Yet you won't
      Let me get away...
         (From you)

So let me go
        That I might be,
A happy soul
        One that is free

To live a life
        Of simplicity
Where I exist
        Yes, me...
    (Without you)-
Either you
        Will let me go
And allow me
        The space to grow
Or I will seek
        A place to hide,
That secret place is...

        SUICIDE!!!!

        (Good Bye to you)

Change
By: Katerria "Starr" Doty

Promise me you'll never change......
You can't, change is inevitable
One constantly evolves,
Ever wonder why relationships have walls
That are often hard to fall
Could it be we haven't spent enough time?
Learning who's we are and whom we are
Is it safe to say the way to remain?
In a state of togetherness,
1 must evolve with the likeness of 1 another

Change is inevitable....
Seasons change
Although we are given signs and symbols
Before change occurs
Before winter we see leaves falling
From trees until they are bare
An unhappy mate will begin to disassociate,
Life will throw you a curve ball
That will make you question all
All things must change, change is needed,
Think of the hurtful change
As that thorn that helps you
With knowing and produces you in growing

Change is inevitable....
Once things were no longer anymore
Body changes, looks alter
As time rolls by and so do we
Once tight skin
Somehow over time looks like
An upside down grin

Think about squirrels in the fall
They have little time for play
They're working hard to find food
To store away
For those cold winter days

Promise me
You'll never change....
I can't
Change is inevitable

THANK YOU
By: Kelly Clark

Thank you LORD
Thank you God
For creating
Women and men
Redeeming us
From our sin

Thank you Earth
Thank you Air
For giving me all I need
To live, to grow and to succeed

Thank you Mom
Thank you Dad
For raising me the best you can
Even if I was not in your plan

Thank you Siblings
Thank you Friends
For being there through it all
Helping me recover
Whenever I fall

Thank you Hard "Aches"
Thank you Struggle
For having your Stronghold
You've matured me a Hundredfold.

Thank you "Myself"
Thank you I
For learning that Love, Hope, Faith
And Action is the keys
Now "We" can rejoice
At the growth in "Me"

HE

By: Lenita McCullor

You wanna be that chick, but you not that chick, trying to play mommy with his kids by his first daughters mother thinking it's gonna make him stick. Stop it ma. Get some self-esteem ma, don't you realize that you a Queen ma?

But she can't because that little head got her going, she sprung on his looks, infatuated with his swag, consume with broken promises, no purpose and no drive.

Life without him couldn't be and staying connected to nothing that possibly could be something. See I know I can make his life worth something, because she's caught up on the potential she sees, that makes her partially feel like this is where she should be.

Wake up ma and stop the fantasies in your mind because in the end you're the one running out of time. That's right! Time doesn't wait on no one!

Unlock the chains off your eyes and stop allowing disrespect to be your guide; waiting on him to love you is imaginable because he's laughing at you on the inside.

Speechless
By: Brenda L. Stovall

I have nothing to say
Because I have no tongue
I have no voice
No opinion
No choice

No rights
No ground to stand
Because I'm a woman
And not a man

Because I'm Black
Because I'm a Child
Because I was a Felon
Because I was Wild

I can't vote
I'm just an "X"
With all of these Amendments
What will be next?

I'm not rich enough
Or in the right class
Soon we'll be like India
The New American Caste
Home of the Proud
Land of the Free
Everyone has a voice
Except me

A Father's Lament
By: Ken Alison

There are my babies too"
When she was born
Problems we had our share
But she had a mother and father
Who loved her and cared....
We put aside our differences
And put our mutual love to work
Our lovely daughter had the best of both worlds
A mother and father to nurture her
And shield her from life's hurt

When he was born
Two parents were there
Mom bringing him forth
Father presents doing his share
Problems were still present
They had aged
The father's addiction the mothers rage
Neither were perfect two sides to their story
But their son was safe and needed not to worry

In the aftermath of their births
Mother and fathers relationship has ended
Fences torn down
Holes never mended
But the children they both love should not have to choose
It seems you've forgotten
They're my babies too!

Children need to be taught
Independence and common sense
They must learn to make decisions
That's in their best interest

They must learn to make decisions
That's in their best interest
Most lessons and role models exist
And come from their environment
When mom and dad are the residents
 So I made a decision
 After hurting you and making so many mistakes
To show them even apart
When it came to them
Their best interest is never at stake

We were in love
We argued, we couldn't always say I'm sorry
But we both took turns
Assuring them there was no need to worry
They had a mother and father
Who loved them far more than their love for each other?
And when things get rough

They can turn to either one or both till things blew over
They belong to you- they belong to me
No matter how divided
We are still thanks to them.....family
Their birthdays, Thanksgiving graduation,
Failing- certificates of accomplishments
Their first visit from the fairy God mother,

Their disappointments-triumphs, epiphanies, bruised ego!
Bandaged knees -sting of love (that's a hard one there)
Loss of a friend bad news, Easter, two weeks visit with me,
Back to you ...conversations about the birds and the bees...
Santa Clause and Christmas
The subtle clue I want to share all these things with them
See I'm their father and they're my babies too!!

HOW DO I LOVE THEE
By; Kelly Clark

How do I love thee?
Let me count the ways
I know everything you do
I know the number of your days

I know the hairs on your head and the tears you cry
I know the day you'll wed and the day you'll die
I know your thoughts and intents
All your reasons why
I separate bone from marrow; the truth from a lie

I see you through your day and I see you through your
night
Watching over you is truly
My sincere delight
For I created you in my image and for My own pleasure
And I will protect and provide for my most valuable
treasure

How do you love ME?
Let me count the ways
For I AM the JUDGE
I know the numbers of your days

Generational Youth

To The Children
By: Ken Alison

Remember young black man child
I was once like you
Buck wild running free
Happy to be alive
Living in the land of the free
No ambition yet!
Full of hope of what I would become, whatever it is,
I would be the best cause I was a bad son of a gun
Remember young black woman
That your mother b4 u
And grandmother b4 her
Was fine, beautiful intelligent by far destined to be a
success B4 the back seat of a car.
Your young gifted and black
A queen of a nation on the rise,
The look of love we sing about is the look that's in your
eyes.
Please don't take this gift of life 4 granted
Treasure every moment that you live
Forget not that 2 whom much is given
There's so much more that you're expected to give

Support

JoAnn Wesley Hassler

I should give myself
The kind of support
I give my friends
I should listen hard
To my own Words
Feelings—Pain
I should make time
To support—Cradle
Encourage—Love
This scarred little girl
Who feels embarrassed?
Too old—to unsure
Too Frightened to
Support Herself

Wake Up!
By: Lenita McCullor

I don't have the hiccups...
I'm trying to purge your thoughts
With hyssop
Combining your time with a glass of wine
That makes you cry
When you see that time
Has passed you by

What happen to Big Mama?
With the switches and belts
And her long talks telling you
"You better get yourself together!"
She gave looks that can kill
And would make you cry,
Now y'all need the help.

What happen to
"Look to the hills for which cometh my help!"
Scriptures you use to speak to me
When I was desperately
Going through intensively

ELDERS we need you...
Where are the role models
Besides what Comcast and Direct TV provide?
The Last Sheep is crying,
Who gone wake up Judah,
Cause we dying,

We sleep to the beat
And our appetite is not even discreet
Cause we're craving for the wrong meat.
Where are the uncles and aunts who cared?
Where are the true teachers & counselors?
Are you still there?

Where are the neighbors who would discipline you &
Would tell your parents what she had to do!
Fathers, Fathers your kids need you,
It's time to get off that "Willie Lynch Train"
And quit cocaine
Then get back into position
Where were you
From the beginning

You hear me, from the beginning.
It's time to take what was
Killed, destroyed and stolen cause
ELDERS, ELDERS, ELDERS
You're needed and you're important.

We Bow Down & Worship...him?
By: Brenda L. Stovall

Baby girl let me tell you now
Watch out for them knees
And for whom you'll bow
Because if it's not the Father
Or for the Son
My Heavenly Father
The Holy One

You're bowing down
To the wrong thing
That's why that Brotha
Won't give you a ring

He doesn't respect you
He'll put you down
He tells his friends
"Homie, she's a clown!"

Who are you worshipping?
To whom are you giving the praise?
Instead of lifting Holy Hands
Only his EGO is raised?
High hopes is what she got
A lot of love, I say NOT!

Because if he loves you
You don't have to do those things
He will honor your vessel
Treat you like a Queen

Who reigns by his side
Not on the floor
Don't let him slide
You're not a whore

It makes me angry
It makes me scrimmage
You're bowing down
To the false image

That can send you
To an early grave
Throat filled with Cancer
Body filled with Aids

That's not the Cream of the Crop
Nor Crème de la Crème
You can't even pray
To Elohim

You got it Twisted Sistah,
You betta get it straight
Repent right now
Before it's too late

And whenever you have
(That desire)
To kneel down
And feel the fire

Not from lust
But from love
From the Heavenly Father
Up above

He won't choke you
Or force nothing in
Shout Hallelujah
He'll forgive your sins

He'll give you the desires
Of your heart
Begin again
This is a brand new start

You won't have to worry
About your car note
Working on that job
And believe this quote

Ask, seek & knock
Can you believe this?
That's all it takes
Here's a Holy Kiss

God is so jealous
He won't answer a man's prayers
If he disrespects you
Or touches a single hair

So respect yourself
Do you have a clue?
Abnormal Use
Is called "abuse"

That's not God's
Purpose for you
Chew on His Word
And do what it do!

Hey Young Girl
By: Katerria "Starr" Doty

At first you were
"Daddy's Girl"
Why did u have to go?
And ruin your world

Selling your soul
Losing all control
Looking for love,
    Using your body
Not your mind and soul

You were so accustomed
To once gold
Now your S.H.I.Q.
Is all old

Fresh into your teen years
Sweet sixteen
    Doesn't mean a thing
To the guys around the way
They all know they
Don't have to pay

To get a piece
You little dummy!
Now your reputation is shot
And your all stressed out
                Hey young girl...

You see I tried to save you,
From that boy who said
He loved you

I knew the plan he had
In store for you
So many female fans....
Sad thing is
    You weren't even in
        His future plans

So now you got this baby
And you ain't even ready
When you called the new dad
To tell him of his now new future
The 1st question to land was.....
        "Are you sure that's my baby?"

So young and all alone
It's so cold when the night grows old
When that baby cries,
U have to go dry those eyes
All the while wishing... daddy was near

Oohhhhhh! So now you fear being a teenage mother
When in the beginning, I tried to warn you
But all you wanted to do was just...
Fit in with your crew
Hey young girl...
    I bet now you
        Have a clue

HEY!

Kelly Clark

Hey little girl
What you gonna do?
Your stomach's poking out
And your boyfriend left you.

Hey little boy
Were you caught with that gun?
Now you're going to jail,
And need your records expunged.

Slow down little kids!
Shouldn't you be in school?
Don't start any fights!
Don't be a fool!

Mind your manners!
Do what is right!
Don't grow up to soon!
Learn to **READ** and to **WRITE!**

REACHING YOUR GOAL
BY: ADRIENNE BRUCE

Remember when you were excited,
Interested and eager to be
Setting out to reach that goal
Designed especially for you
As time went on you learned how to
Persevere,
Weather the storm and
Meet all challenges head on
Several times you looked back and
Realized how far you had come.
Sometimes it wasn't easy or even fair.
There was difficulty you had to bare
Many times it was smooth sailing
Accomplishments felt real good
No, it would not have been wise to quit
You were half way through it
Just one more step, one more hurdle
One giant leap

This is an appointment

You will have to keep

Reach out and grab it, hang on tight
Grab this goal with all your might
You've earned it, it's yours,
And you have the right.
When you grab it,
Embrace it,
Enjoy it,
Face it.
But do not savor the moment to long
Because there is something else
You will have to do

You must set your next goal,

It awaits you.

GENERATIONS: LEGACY
By Linda D. Gaddis

How do you wish to be remembered?

As a shooting star
    Or a dying ember?
As a raging sea
    Or a calming breeze?
As an apple tree
    Or a wilting leaf?
As a majestic eagle
    Or a common sea gull
As an exotic flower
    Or a dilapidated tower?
As a jeweled crown
    Or a hand-me-down
As a pair of Jimmy Choos
    Or Dunlap Shoes.
As an incurable romantic
    Or a sadistically fanatic?

There are many ways to be remembered you see.
    So think how you want your legacy.

Generational Elder

The Collection

By: JoAnn Wesley Hassler

I think of myself as a non-collector...
Never a fan of small ceramic figurines, expensive
artwork, plates to hang on the wall,
Nevertheless...

I have too many books
Some read, some waiting
Love of reading, even as a library patron
Checking out ten or fifteen books
Satisfies my curiosity

Perusing my favorite resale shops
Several times a month
Often leaving with a bargain of two...
Unable to resist a three dollar t-shirt,
Or a ten dollar pair of fancy heels
Someone else's cast off,
Now my new treasure
Am I a Collector?

I accumulate travel opportunities
Line pearls on a string
Choosing, savoring and recollecting experiences
Culture and travel companions
Upon which to reminisce and re-enjoy
At a future date...
Am I a Collector?

I amass classes
On everything from work related to
Mind expanding and creative
Blissful in a classroom
As teacher or student,
Delighted on either side of the desk...
Am I a Collector?

I collect friends
Who is ever a stranger?
Satisfying a deep desire to connect, expand, and
Go deeply into the diverse human experience...
Am I a Collector?

I may be collecting grandchildren...
Ten and counting...
Five girls and five boys
Each enriches my soul with their possibility
Their yet unknown contribution
To the world
And to the future...
I am a part of their DNA,
They are my legacy...
Am I a Collector?

I collect journals, my writing,
My record of the days of my life
Perhaps upon my death, of interest to no one
But to me, the recording gives significance...
Each day gratefully lived,
Facing challenges and delight;
The tapestry of life...
Am I a Collector?

In the end, I know I am
A High Extrovert
The blessing and curse ...
I do not want to miss anything,
Anyone,
Any experience...
I want to fill up and be filled
Live life to its very borders...
Am I a Collector?

Each day
A blank canvas
To be filled with experiences,
People, challenges, opportunities
I do not want to live an unlived life...

Title of a book I once read,
I want to expand and embrace
Each collected experience
Regret will come only
In what I have rejected, ignored
Or have escaped my notice

What I collect is not what one puts on a shelf
Gathering dust and needing to be dusted.
But what one surrounds herself with
Creating a full and meaningful life
The life of a writer, matriarch, reader, friend,
Lifelong learner and citizen of the world...
A life filled with juicy collections.

I'm Still Standing!
By: Brenda L. Stovall

My eyes may be dim
But I can see
All of the changes
Inside of me

I used to run, walk
And be spry
Now I'm lucky
If I can cook a pie

Oh child, I had a walk
That made men whistle
Got arthritis and gout right now
I can't find it even with a missile

Perky breast that stood
Up At attention
I'm lucky these days
If I get an honorable mention

Cold wavy hair
That was black as coal
It's silvery white
Signs that I am old

They say "Black don't crack!"
But I got a few wrinkles
Age spots, crow's feet
And even some dimples

But I wouldn't trade this
For a thing
My life is like a tree
With many rings

That's rooted in love
No longer stumped by life
Age old wisdom
I have the Tree of Life

Whose Bark is not sharp
You know I can't bite
Ha, ha, Because I have to take
My teeth out a night

But my branches
Stretch far and wide
Hugs and kisses for my Grands
They give me such pride

You see I'm blessed
To have made it this age
A hoary head says the bible
Is a sign I'm smart...a great stage!

So as I
Mosey along
Come walk with me
And sing this song

Today is such
A beautiful day
Air in my lungs
To the Lord I pray

I have my right mind
I don't have dementia
Can't tie my shoes but got feet
No teeth but got dentures

I chew on his word
And pray at night
I'm thankful to God
I appreciate life

Shout to the mountains
I have no fear
I'm thankful to God
I'm here another year!

Elders
By: Ken Alison

When I was young
I thought that forty and fifty
Years of age was old

I was always scared
That my parents and other elders
Of my family would die
Because that's what old people do

But now that I'm an elder
I realize that life is
A gift to the young as well as the old

And that elders
Has a responsibility
As well as a commitment
To teaching the young to live life

One day at a time
And that death takes no prisoners
Young or old

GENERATIONS: LOOK AT ME
Linda D. Gaddis

Look at my hands
The nails no longer shine
Like they did last time
Look at my feet
The toes they curl
And darken nail.
Look at my eyes
They luster lack
And cataract
Look at my face
It saddens me
At what I see
Lines of despair
Are everywhere
Look at my head
My darkened hair
Has much gray
And silver will soon be on its way
So take this for
What its worth
Father time and Mother Earth
Will only let you stay
So many hours of a day
Before you are called away

Take care of you
Please...take care of you!

"Mid Thirty Blues"
By: Katerria "Starr" Doty

Pressured by the woes of life
I'm in and outta this funk
Congested my mind, with the cares of life
Multi-tasking all the days long

Thinking about those days being in my twenty + 2's
Sh#@...think back, please take a moment....go back with
me
Spring hen or rooster sowing oats
Living foot loose and fancy free
Days of hanging out all night
Able to bounce back, going to the gig with fresh wig
From just last night

In and outta town, no time for being bound,
Life was grand 100 grand
And you'd better believe, I kept a tan
Twenty +2's, you couldn't lose
We were in our prime, time to grind, and of course
unwind

Most things done in those twenty + 2's have to be
undone
These now thirty + 2's is a different time,
A shift must now take place
Darn it young blood! Enjoy because life is going to
happen
Mid Thirty Blues, these down right, maxed out, sour
mood Blues...

Mid Thirty Blues...Is this the blues?
Or the testing point to see if you'll win or lose,
Live or die
Not natural death, but spiritually
Is this the point where life hits you at many angles to
see?
If you'll fold
Or will you be bold, will you stand till you reach that
Pot of gold
Or that rainbow that always shines after the storms of
life
Passes 1 by
Mid Thirty Blues, these down rite, maxed out, sour
mood Blues...

Am I being stripped of everything giving to me?
In return starting over on my own
They say its better the 2nd time around
I reckon its best I get off this merry-go-round
Move forward pick up the pieces
Pieces of my dream, your dream move forward
Don't be insane mane, doing the same thing, the same
way and Expecting a different way
Yahweh the true way

Starting over on my own huh
I need my mojo back, not my back thrown out,
But my swiftness back
Back in tha' day when I was young
I'm not a kid anymore
Can I have my Savior back?
My favor back!

Keep on moving! Don't stop!
Only look back to remind you of that sting that set you
back
It got your attention for recognition
But they say...hey, hey, the blues is alright
But it hurts, it really hurts
Is this the blues? Mid Thirty Blues
These down right, maxed out, sour mood
Blues.....

HEY YOUNG WORLD
By: Lenita McCullor

Without history where would we be...?
Without knowing the struggle
That our forefathers and civil rights leaders
Had to endure to achieve
A piece of this American Dream
That's still being robbed by thieves

Without history...
How would you know?
What you can do
With the abilities and strength
That's within you,
Knowing your history is the key
In understanding why I am
Who I am

White! White has blacked out
And deceived you when I speak the truth!
It's hard for your mind to unwind because lies
Have consumed you and is seated in the core of you.
Because of the white out,
Your history is now a hidden treasure,
But I promise you, if you seek, you shall find,
If you knock the door shall be open
Hey young world, history is important.

BLACK HISTORY
By: Kelly Clark

Africa is the continent where it all began
Genesis, the **Pyramids**, the first **Humans**.
Great **abundance, wealth** and **riches**
Were provided for us to share
Mount Kilimanjaro, Lake Victoria and
The **Great Rift Valley** is there.

We were **Kings** and **Queens**
Adorned with crowns, sepulchral and golden rings
Ruling kingdoms, dynasties, villages, tribes and things
Then slavery came and spoiled the land
Pillage rape and theft of resources and clan.

For some the Atlantic Ocean was their final destination
For others, they would endure even
greater degradation.
King crops, plantations, lynchings and beatings
No rights, auction blocks and Ku Klux Klan Meetings.

The North against the South!
Civil War! Slaves freed!!
Abe died! We cried, but survived
And now we can Read!!

Reconstruction, Renaissance, Rosa Parks,
Martin Luther King
Civil Rights, Assassinations, New Deal,
Marion Anderson Sings!
Now, Chisholm runs for president

And Hip Hop flares
Affirmative Action, Jessie Jackson,
Oprah Winfrey Airs.

Later Rodney King cries
"Can We All Just Get Along?"
Lois Farrakhan marches on Washington,
One million men strong!

Colin Powell and Condoleezza Rice
Moved up in political value
While Denzel Washington and Halle Berry
Took home the Oscar Statue

Then people became disillusioned
And wondered where are black leaders had went
When Chicago Senator Barack Obama became
Our **44th President!!**

Time moves on and we still need work
But "**Our history**" **is up to us!**
We must **Stand Together** stop complaining **and Work!**
Or be back on the back of the bus.

Our Future is Bright!
We can make a change if we have faith
And if we believe
We Can reverse years of slavery,
Poverty, ignorance and disrespect
With Honor,
Then **We Will Receive!**

Plenty Prayers to be Prayed
Adrienne Bruce

If you think you have nothing to pray
Pray about what's going on
In the world today
There's plenty prayers to be prayed

Families have been evicted
With nowhere to go
Young children scared,
Homeless and hungry
Numerous babies, aborted legally
Men sexual abusing
Young innocent boys
Plenty prayers to be prayed

A patient finds out
They have terminal cancer
Dad has just been laid off
His job, no explanation
A terrified mother reports
Her teenage daughter missing
Aids epidemic sweeping the country
Wars are fought
For what?
Who really knows?
Plenty prayers to be prayed

Young virgin girl
Raped by family member
Drugs being sold and brought
In all neighborhoods
A little boy waiting
For a heart transplant
A cure needed for
Herpes, AIDS, and Cancer
Rocket ships blowing up
On the way to the moon
Plenty more prayers need to be prayed

Passenger planes flying
Into world's tallest buildings
Drive by shootings killing
Whose ever is in the way
Alcohol is being consumed
By the fifth everyday
Vows of marriage broken
By illicit sexual affairs
Bribes and pay-offs accepted
By politicians who say they care
Plenty more prayers to be prayed

One man kills his entire family
Kid attacked by pit bull
Suburban Mayor owes back taxes
Lotto jack pot in the millions
Get rich quick, that's not the way
Quick drop to your knees let's pray
Plenty more prayer to be prayed

Pain, Suffering, and Mental Disease
Don't forget to pray for these
Prayer can make a difference
In our lives today
The Lord really listens
To what we have to say
Let's start to pray
For what's on this list
And any other request
We may have missed

Bow your head
We need to start right away
Dear Lord we have
Plenty prayers to be prayed

Historical
"His Story"

FAMILY PORTRAIT
By: Linda D. Gaddis

My President
The First Family
They are four
I am one
They are me
I am they
Simplistic attire
Yet fitting

Joyous occasion
Big smiles
Acknowledge the moment
And in that moment,
A family unites
Themselves and their country

Color coordinated
Family generated
Nationally motivated
Globally situated
To demonstrate
The power

Which is possessed
 By this man
  His family...
   His faith in family
    Self & Nation

That's HIS Story
By: Kelly Clark

Before the
Red White and Blue
The Land of the
Red Black and Green
Graced the scene

Predating that, David was King.
Taking us to the days of Solomon
History is just hollow son-
Without the days of yester year
Reappearing on our pages
Painting the picture
As the world changes
From slavery to bravery

Brothers and Sisters claiming the modern times stop
the tape and press rewind as we our ancestry in
Book where it is written; let's not forget the days that
were paved for even Sojourner Truths to speak on a
better way.
Sojourner Truth, Naomi and Ruth, Deborah bringing
back the head of the beast, proving she was chief
And fast-forward to the Underground Railroad where
Harriet took hold of the captive to make free.

Before then we had Esther standing before the King!
African Cultures, Hebrew History....Black people...It is
written...it's not hidden...It's not a mystery.
That HIS-Story is our Story
Rising and making legacy.
Cause as HE rise, we rise
And all else is history.

Dr. King walked the streets
Israel walked on bare feet.
Gods laws kept, Mans law changed...to see better days.
Equal rights...equally we fight.
Willie Lynch, Jim Crow...Slavery abolished fo'sho...
But what'dya know...History repeats itself
Repeat the Word of God...Don't keep it to yo-self
Live the Legacy...He breathed breath in me...

I am Black History.

Hail To The Chief
By: Ken Alison

The morning after the election
Before the fact that history had been made
My first thought when I opened my eyes was
Of all the graves that had been filled by the deaths of
visionary and soldiers for the destiny to be fulfilled
Before I knew how long you had been committed to your
wife your children your faith.

Your vision I thought about all the possibilities that you
certainly had to entertain concerning the reaction to
the reality that you a man of color would occupy the
house of white on Philadelphia ave. in Washington D.C.
I thought about the poor little boys and girls who could
no longer say with affirmation that this dream would
never come true

A black man like me, a black woman like u....
HAIL TO THE CHIEF AND OUR FIRST LADY!

I've Got That Picture Hanging On My Wall
By: Katerria "Starr" Doty

The 1st family,
Now were all in the family melody?
Better be!
Did we ever think we'd see this day?
For sure
We've got a piece of real life history
It's no longer his-story but actual history, all white
I smite that's just a white lie
We'll shout from the mountain top
Even our folks over in Africa and Hawaii say
We're sho nuff bout cha
We could even Cha-Cha slide
With our President from tha Chi
Shoot some ball, Ballroom dance,
He always takes a stand and shows our young brothers
All about swag, and never does he brag
Oh, yes we can ...yes we can!
Yes we did!
Malcolm, Martin, Mary McLeod Bethune, Harriet,
W.E.B. DeBois, Langton Hughes, Emmitt Till
'Till we meet again
Yes we can,
Yes we will,
Yes we did,
Yes we'll do it again!

A Love for Black
By: Brenda L. Stovall

We pray all day
And cry all night
We Can't find no husbands
That will treat us right

Several thousand children
With the big head
Another generation
Half past dead

Some shaking it fast
Others dropping it
Like it's hot
J lo with Halo's
While brothers carrying glocks

With their pants on the ground
Others reaching for soap
Others fooling around
Slinging that dope

Some on the "D.L."
That means "down low"
They just low down
And to white women
They go

Is it our mouths?
Is it our hair
Is it our desires
Of wanting you there

As our husbands
Not your "baby's mama"
Child support checks
It's too much drama

My heart aches
For the old school
black man
Who loved his children
And did all he can

To make it work
And worked all day
Took his family to church
And on his knees he prayed

Where are the Martins
Where are the Kings
Where are you Malcolm
What happened to the dream

Brothers wearing suits
Who respected their mothers
Cleaned and shined their shoes
And dressed like no other

Tailored made
Tried and true
Clean fingernails
And never rude

They tipped their hats
And opened doors
Not only for women
But for you and more

Where are the Langstons
We come in many hues
Dizzy Gillespie
B.B. Singing the blues

Where are the Black
Renaissance Men
The writers and poets
Even Gil Scott-Heron

We used to be killed
If we read or write
Can't we pick up a book
And fight for our rights

Thurgood Marshall
W.E.B. Dubois
It's time to fight
And reclaim our boys

Hey our warriors
Put your weapons down
Stop fighting each other
And look around

So we won't lose
Or have to save face
For the extinction of
Our Beautiful Black Race

Family Memories
By: Lenita McCullor

This is a long lasting legacy of love, all of our
offspring's are here and I'm holding these pictures
wishing our Father would've gave our deceased one's
more years, but your spirit is here. The mood is just
right and the atmosphere is pleasant.

We are all gathering at this dynamic cookout at my
parents' house. Greeting everybody with kisses and
hugs and the thug cousins always show love. Mama
Barbequing and dad preaching and teaching as he always
do.

Joseph and Jerome don't have a clue, of how much love
I really have for you. I see Auntie Joyce bringing that
six pack of Miller's in and sneaking Toot a can. The card
table is set and Uncle Nate and I is about to checkmate
Kathy and Kay in this game of spades.

Now there's a lot of fussing and cussing because the
sore losers can't hang. All snap the doorbell just rang.
Liz and Ty are sweaty and hot but I thank God they
came. These are family memories that you can't get
back! These are my people and I want them all to know
that I love them in spite of the small and pity brawls we
have.

Sammy, my baby, keep taking it one day at a time and I believe you gone make it. Clara never let go of your dreams because one day, it's going to be a reality for you and your team. The kids are scattered in the backyard playing jump rope and basketball. It's just family and I'm loving them all.

Auntie Jackie keep doing you and remember that God hasn't forgot the plans he has for you; to the rest of y'all this poem is written for you to. I care about each and every last one of you. So let this legacy of love continue and don't forget that I L.O.V.E you.

Love & Black History Goes a Long Way
By: Adrienne Bruce

Love and **Black History** is celebrated the same month. Have you really thought about it?
We seriously need to Fall in LOVE with **Black History**. How important are our roots? The past got us to the present and the present will takes us to our futures. Now is the time to embrace the struggles, pain, and anguish our ancestors suffered.

It was purposeful and necessary for **African Americans** today to enjoy their freedoms. Yes, we have come a long way from the water hosing, dog attacks, lynching's, crazy bus rides, restaurant sit-ins, special water fountains, school denials, no voting rights, not able to express ourselves with a whistle or gather publicly. WOW! We couldn't really do much. Being a servant was top job. Cleaning houses, performing nanny duties and factory work was a means of financial support. This wasn't that long ago if you think about it.

Look at the job title today **Blacks** hold CEO's, entrepreneurs, mayors, radio/ TV, announcer, policeman (had to chuckle at that one) and let's not forget the Presidency.
Boy, we as a people have made it to the Promised Land and accomplished goals our relatives set. How proud they would be. Just imagine the smiles on their faces, laughing, clapping full of joy, saying "We did it! We fought a good fight!"

I often think about the timing of my birth. I get to enjoy many freedoms today and I dare not forget the price that was paid. I may it my responsibility to teach the youth about the African American struggle and how grateful they should
be. So to all millennial African Americans, please don't forget to celebrate the struggle of your great grandmothers, grandfathers, fourth generation aunts and uncles, distant cousins, and all others who stood for your freedoms today.

At your next family reunion, give them all a big hug and wrap them in LOVE and say "Thanks for the path you paved for me", especially before you eat that slice of mouth watering Pound Cake from which the Recipe was passed down from previous generations.

Short **Stories**

The Reluctant Marathoner
JoAnn Wesley Hassler

Completing a marathon was never on my short list. I went to Catholic school in the 1950's; we did not even have recess. Women's athletics were not a part of my growing up. When I was in high school, whenever we had a difficult PE class like tumbling, I had warts removed so I did not have to participate. No one seemed to catch on and I was able to use this excuse many times in four years.

At age 35, however, I began walking for exercise. My ex-husband completed his first marathon at age 50. I became his cheerleader, driver and encourager as he participated in one race after another. As I stood at the finish line, I became aware that a significant number of the runners did not exactly look like Olympic athletes. At age 50, I decided to join him not as a runner but as a walker. The Disney Marathon in Orland had an extended finish time of seven hours. This accommodated a 15 minute mile which was although challenging, walk friendly.

The marathon for me was a part of an elaborate celebration of my 50th birthday. It was a busy year; I did not begin training until October. Three days a week, I walked from 9-12 through the streets and subdivisions of Naperville. It was a beautiful fall and the walks were lovely.

My companions were WGN radio hosts Kathy O'Malley and Judy Markey, however, as will happen in a Chicago winter, the good weather gave way to cold winter. I then resorted to what I know was a taste of hell. I walked on a treadmill in my health club for three hours at a time. It perfectly personified eternal damnation: doing the same activity over and over and going nowhere forever and ever amen.

In January, brand new Nikes in hand and "*Just Do It*" emblazoned across my chest, Don and I arrived in Orlando ready to participate in a marathon together for the first time. The morning of the race, was at the back of the pack with the other walkers; Don was a bit further up. Along the way, there were bystanders on the sideline who would encourage, clap and wish us well just as I had done all those years for Don.

One such memorable sideline encourager was a large man in a red shirt who made eye contact with me clapped loudly and said, "Stay Strong!" I have never forgotten him; whenever I send an encouraging note to someone who running a marathon, facing a challenge or going through a hard time or I encourage them to Stay Strong.

At mile twelve the photographer took my picture. That was a lucky break because at mile 16 with blisters that felt like balloons, I knew I could not walk another 10.2 miles. I acquiesced, came off the route and was bused to the finish line. It was a huge disappointment. Once again from the sidelines, I watched Don come across the finish line, get his medal from Donald Duck and enjoy another victory.

Fast Forward: 10 years later.

My beloved god daughter, Becky, was diagnosed with breast cancer at age 28; no family history whatsoever. We were all shocked. We supported in every way we could think of. My daughter, Julie is six months younger than Beck and her best friend. She saw an advertisement about the Avon 2 Day Walk for Breast Cancer. With her encouragement and a bit of trepidation, I agreed to join her.

At first I was a bit concerned about the fund raising but decided I could make up the difference myself if need be. My greatest concern, however, was finishing what I had been unable to do ten years before. This time, I reached out for help. I made an appointment with a Podiatrist who suggested Nikes would never have worked for me in the first race. They run too narrow and no one should wear new shoes the day of a race.

She instructed me to go to a good running shoe store and be fitted by a professional. She further suggested should buy two pair of shoes that were a size larger to accommodate swelling and alternate them during training. For the race I was to bring both pair and wear the second pair the second day and several pairs of good socks. I followed her instructions to the letter; I needed all the help I could get!

The Avon walk was in the June, spring training was easier than training in the fall; I could train right up to the weekend before the event. This time I did not have to walk for hours indoors on the dreaded tread mill. In addition, these 26.2 miles did not have the 7 hour time constraint. All I needed to do was *stay strong* and keep walking. I also had an accountability partner in Julie.

The day of the race I was so nervous I missed most of the opening ceremony waiting in line for the porta-potty. I reached mile 16 with blisters once again. This time, I headed for the First Aid tent, had the blisters broken, moleskin applied, changed my socks and continued on. At mile 20, I knew I was going to finish; I started to cry. Julie was ahead of me setting the pace. She turned, saw my tears and said, "No crying...it takes too much energy." 6.2 miles later arm and arm we crossed the finish line with Becky in our hearts.

We were further challenged that evening as we struggled with and finally had to ask for assistance in putting up our tent. We are not campers! We brought a queen sized blow up mattress; the night was cold and we slept cuddled close together like we did when she was a little girl.

The next day we walked the 13.1 miles and we were not at the at the back of the pack. As we sat on the grass at the finish line watching the other walkers coming in, I reflected on the sense of satisfaction I felt accomplishing my goal of finishing not only a marathon but another half marathon the next day.

The victory was short lived, however, as I also reflected on the fact that my challenge was over, but Becky and thousands others would wake up that day and every day henceforth with the challenge of fighting and with cancer. I watched the family members and friends of breast cancer survivors, those who lost loved ones and the survivors themselves crossing the finish line.

I knew what made the difference this time for me and for others who questioned their ability to finish this challenge was that they were doing it for a higher purpose. We all did it to raise money for breast cancer research. We had a goal beyond ourselves, beyond our personal ego. We walked to raise money with the hope of finding a cure for this terrible disease.

Fast forward: Five years later...

Becky froze her eggs before she went through Chemo. She is now the proud mother of two year old twins: Ben and Kate. Julie also started her family and has two young sons. They are still best friends and living out their childhood dream of raising their children together. The Avon Breast Cancer Two Day takes place in Chicago in early June. Each year thousands walk for the cure.

SNAPPER
By: Ken Alison

When I first met her she was given to me for free. The woman who introduced us was much older than me. I was struggling to recover from a marriage and relationship gone badly. I'd be the first to admit it was the most none plus thrill id ever had.

The older woman was wise and knew she had to slow me down because my youth was too much for her to handle, but she wanted me around. The carnal things she taught me for a young man pure delight. She said I'd never 4get her and 38 years later darn it if she wasn't right!

Some years went by before I met her again. This time it was a friend who sold it to acquaintances and friends. She was sold in a pony pack $25 a lick. Some girls who couldn't afford her enjoy her with a trick. She was status quo if u knows what I mean. To participate in her pleasure meant you were part of the scene. She came pure, cut, and in liquid. You snort it, lick it, or mix it in a drink. The allure was simple pleasure the side effect more than you'd think.

Then a friend came home from Cali, he took an early morning flight. In his bags he bought packages that would change our whole lives. You see we didn't know you could cook it not to eat but put it in a pipe and smoke it. Free- base but she was no longer free. One by one he lined us up made us squat- standing up as we took a hit, and 1 by 1 we proclaimed that's some bad s.h,i.q.!

Our futures at the time were bright we were upcoming stars and our stars lit up the night. We had no idea wed embraced the devil for this girl was something else, and she turned us all inside out till we were shells of our former selves. 1 by 1 we felt our souls destined for hell some would not live long enough their stories someone else would have to tell.

It's been almost 40 years since that older woman who turned me out and introduced me to her friend, her name id never forget the pain of the pain... see that girl I met nearly 40 years ago her name was Cocaine.

Challah Anwar Hall
By: Lenita McCullor

On January 1, 2007 I received a phone call from my father at 9:47am. I quickly wished him Happy New Year's, assuming that's what the call was about. It was twenty seconds of silence on the phone and in a calm tone my dad said Lenita, your Mother and I are at Jackson Park hospital with your brother Challah. I was nervously afraid to ask what's going on with him. My dad begin telling me that he didn't have all the information, and all he knew was that my brother was brought in by ambulance unconscious with a stab wound in his chest and another in his side.

Not too long after my parents were anxiously waiting to see their son, the doctor walked out to the waiting room and removed his white mask that had clutched his face. My Dad said his expression was so devastating that we just knew it was bad news! My mom and Dad fell to the floor when they heard the words sorry it was nothing we could do. Immediately I dropped the phone and yelled until I couldn't yell anymore. My daughter frantically ran to the living room and asked me what was wrong. While still crying and in unbelief of what was told to me, I told her to "put some clothes on, we got to go"!

As I arrived at the hospital I could see my family members in huddles crying and some in silence. I began asking for my mother and the nurse directed me to where she was. When I saw her I wanted to kill who killed him because my mother was broken in pieces! Her spirit was torn and at that very moment it seemed as though time had stood still. From there everything was moving in slow motion. The only thing that I was able to do was hug her and love on her without asking how she felt.

The people from the morgue had not yet arrived so I rushed in the room where Challah was. When I saw him I instantly thought about how Jesus raised Lazarus from the dead and I start asking God could he perform the same miracle right now. The room was cool and his eyes were semi open. As I walked close to the bed, I bowed down and kissed his forehead and my lips were cold as his eyes instantly closed fully. I begin crying and asking him "what happened...who did this to you"?

I was actually expecting a response from him. I know that's crazy but that's where my mind was at that time. I kissed him again and left out the room. I went to my parents and began hugging them. My dad was being strong for us, but I could see the rage and anger that penetrated his face. The police and the ambulance were still around. Mama was talking to the paramedics. They asked her did she want to know his final words and she said, "Yes I do". Challah's last words were "I can't breathe, am I going to die...I don't want to die!" The paramedics told him, "you're not going to die" and they continue massaging his heart. His final words were, "yes I am because I can't breathe anymore" and immediately he was unconscious.

The doctors told us that his cause of death was congestive heart failure and five main arteries were ruptured. The detectives began asking questions and told us that his daughter's grandmother had murdered him. We were all in awe and in desperate need for answers. Challah was stab by his girlfriend's mother. My family was ready to kick ass and ask questions later. My sister was blowing up the phone trying to reach Challah's girlfriend, but there was no answer.

I tried to call her a couple of hours later and the story she told me was her mother and sisters were all playing cards and drinking and smoking, having fun getting ready to bring in the New Year. Until this day this is all I know and the story has always been unclear and surreptitious to me. I don't know what escaladed because Carrie never explained what really happened. Carrie told me she saw her mother going into the kitchen and getting a steak knife and proceeding to the bedroom for about thirty-five minutes.

She claimed that everything happened so unexpectedly and before she knew it, my brother was stabbed in the chest and her mother ran out the house. During that time I lived right across the alley where the incident occurred. Carrie told me she immediately got some cold towels and put on his wound, not aware of the severity of it. She began telling me that Challah was making his way to the door, holding on to the wall where his blood was smeared. He made it outdoors grasping for air.

It was one year later when the trial began. Carrie's mother was brought to the courtroom with a smirk on her face. I was still emotionally messed up and mentality stuck. The trial was crazy! It was heavy tension in the courtroom. Sheriffs stood in the middle of the aisles between the families to make sure everything stayed calm. One by one Carrie and her sisters took the stand and nobody seems to remember what happen the night of January 1, 2007.

That really hurt my family and me because we were good to Carrie including Challah. To hear the lies and the cover ups, it really did something to me on the inside. I remember saying, "life is so unfair...why him"! After a few days the verdict really took me by surprise! How in the hell this chick get charged with 2nd degree murder and her release year is 2014! This supposedly justice system is backwards as hell! She took my brother's life and all she receives is 8 years!

I personally think it's a shame that gangbangers who sell drugs receive more time than those who take a life, especially my brother. It was so hard to move on and at that time I truly didn't know how because I never lost someone so close to me. So I went through life internalizing my feelings. I had been carrying this burden for three years until finally I had a breakdown. I began to cry out to God please take this pain from me because I'm hurting and I still miss my brother. I miss his smile, I miss his laughter, I miss the arguments, and I miss him needing my advice.

May 3, 2010, I had a dream that I was looking for my brother and he suddenly appeared at the end of the couch where I slept. I was frantic to see him and I said "the whole family is upstairs waiting on you". Challah said "hey I'm only here to see you". We began telling each other how much we miss and loved one another.

We hugged and I didn't want to let go. This dream seemed so real. Then my baby brother looked me in my eyes and said, "Lenita, it's time to move on with your life" then the image of him faded and disappeared. When I woke up I was laughing, then crying, then laughing, then crying! My emotions were stirred like a pot of soup! As I rose, I felt a burden been lifted! I was free at last! Now, I understand what it means "that there's no sorrow on earth that heaven can't heal".

Smile Still Alive
By: Katerria "Starr" Doty

As days led up to my departure for Europe I couldn't help but wonder what was in store for my eyes to see and experience. Italy and Greece were both a trip of a lifetime. Although times are tough I dare not pass up this opportunity. I've said long ago I plan to travel the world, so here's my start to international travel.

I sacrificed so much; there were bills I just didn't pay. I raided my closet and found many clothes I called my treasures. I prayed for God's blessings in this decision making. If I looked at my current financial stance, there would have been no way I could have gone to Europe for 11 days! So I call this adventure exploring with a spiritual eye. I made a conscience decision to call this vacation my third eye experience.

Regardless of experiences I would use my third eye, my spiritual eye to understand this journey as I travel in air to Italy and on water to Greece and back home in my Wrangler Jeep. Wow, this Swiss plane has three rows of seating 9 seats across. That's right! I'm flying international for the first time! Seven hours to Zurich and a little over an hour to Venice. Many things differ when flying international, like we had individual screens with multiple choices of movies to watch.

We were given choices of wine, alcohol, or other beverages. We were served hot meals and a snack all at no additional cost. The food served I did enjoy after calming down. I watched the flight attendants serve many in front of me till I dosed off to sleep. When I awoke and signaled the attendant, she told me they don't wake people when they sleep nor do they save meals. She found a meal that was different than the one I chose from the menu when purchasing my airline ticket.

Though mildly upset, I just ate it and tried my best to enjoy it. So the good news in that was on the flight home from Italy, I also fell asleep. Upon my waking, people were again finishing meals and before I could speak, the attendant said, "I ran out of meals served but I will be serving you first class meals" and she began telling me of my choices. Might I add the food was great, very flavorful! The veal was sautéed with vegetables, sweet potatoes with a hint of nutmeg, salad that displayed every color of the rainbow, and for dessert, raspberry tart.

My traveling friend and I exited our flight to Zurich and upon boarding our connecting flight to Italy; we noticed his laptop was left on the previous plane. With time running out, he successfully notified the airline of his loss so they could retrieve it. He was told to call tomorrow. If in fact they found it, they would fly his laptop to Venice where we'd have to claim it.

I remained positive using my third eye for these experiences. Yes the next day we were able to retrieve it. Once our plane landed a bit of nervousness settled in my stomach making me feel as if I had to use the bathroom as well as my heart that beated as hard and fast as my brother does when he plays his drums. This was due to the fact that we hadn't yet secured our room for Venice, Italy. As we looked for hotels online for those 3 days before the cruise, the prices were so expensive that I figured we might have to stay at a hostel, or simply rough it.

Either way we were now walking out the door as I saw an information booth. We walked over and asked the lady for assistance on finding a reasonable hotel for our stay in Venice. As she began searching she kept shaking her head left and right which made my heart beat even faster, so fast I was feeling the pressure in my throat. As I wanted her to reassure us, on several occasions she said "Seems all hotels are sold out".

As she said let me try this, after a moment of further searching, surprisingly "Lis Bona" she says. "Lis Bona in San Marco $99 for the night, this room is usually $200 but someone cancelled at the last minute". I asked "is it a nice hotel"? She replied "beautiful hotel and you'll be in the heart of everything...they also serve breakfast. You will have to secure the room here with a deposit of $50".

Walking out of the airport was a breeze now, for we had a comfortable place to sleep. Although we hadn't seen the room for some reason I believed her report. We took a water taxi to San Marco. What a beautiful sight Venice had to offer. Many buildings were old in age but simplified renewed beauty. Most window ledges have fresh flowers hanging from them. After arriving in San Marco we had no idea where to go.

We saw a man standing in the middle of the sidewalk with a dolly. We denied him thinking we could find the hotel on our own. We asked several people where our hotel was, many people told us, but to no avail. We saw the man again and this time we gracefully accepted him to port our luggage to the hotel. We followed this man on foot through alleyways and over bridges till we arrived at *Lis Bona Hotel.* We would have never found that hotel on our own. It took a moment for me to embrace all the beauty and process my reality... I'm in Italy!

The front lobby was bright red and gold in color with such beautiful lamps. Needless to say the artwork gave us a glimpse of what our eyes would see here in Venice. Our room was also red and gold pinstriped wallpaper made from fabric. Plush red carpet was throughout the hotel, so plush each step I took my foot sank to the bottom of the floor and back up with the next step.

Our window was covered by green wooden doors. Once we opened the doors to the windows and looked down, we discovered alleyways covered in water with gondolas. We faced other hotels but the water separated us. Such beautiful sights and sounds! The sound of men using poles to push them through the water by gondolas, while singing in Italian what I would assume are love songs. Lovers and friends using that time to embrace such beauty, it cost nothing to use our eyes and soak in all the multitude of colors from the horizon, beauty in the architecture, live music that traveled over the waters, sounds of water, and most of all the feelings of love being displayed!

The next morning we asked the front desk if we could reserve that or another room, and he apologized they were sold out. So we knew we'd have to look for another hotel, but before all that we sat and enjoyed a good breakfast. All sorts of deli meats and cheese, along with this good croissant with something like honey toasted on top and this prepackaged toasted bread, along with several fresh juices, coffee, and teas of choice. With money being tight and having to make it another day in Venice we decided to take enough to fill our doggie bags. We found the famous rialto bridge and decided to sit alongside and people watch and eat our lunch take pictures and decide our next move.

After exploring San Marco, we stumbled past several hotels that were all sold out. Our last hope, *Best Western Diana,* with 1 room left at $140 for the night. The room was on the third floor in the attic. This room was so small only 1 full sized bed and the dresser holding the television could fit. The bathroom was also small there was only the toilet, sink, and bath. As I looked for the shower I located the shower head over the sink, so this meant everything is done in this space, there was a floor drain in the middle of the floor, the walls and floor had ceramic tile. I'd never seen anything like that before, we opened the windows and saw clay tiled roofs.

We also saw alleyways and cafes through the gaps in buildings. We saw people watering their flowers, sipping their drinks from their mugs, and most of all the night sky was dark blue with white swirls that illuminated the sky. Jehovah Jireh our provider saw that we slept well thus far. We were on our way to the next part of our adventure, Greece that is! At first there was a culture shock. Only 6 African Americans on this entire ship! I wondered just how much fun I'd have.

There were people from everywhere...Moscow, South Africa, UK, England, Saudi Arabia, Argentina, Germany, Dominican Republic, Panama, Netherlands, Columbia, Australia, and other places I'd never heard! So my question was fair, so many languages spoken this was truly a great experience. I'll just sum up the answer to my question; I met some amazing people on that cruise. I gained associates I believe will remain in my life. People were open and we enjoyed one another. It got to be even those who didn't speak English were still communicating with us. There were a couple groups of people we explored Greece with, before long we became a family on the ship. We began eating breakfast together, traveled the four islands of Greece together, dined, visited vineyards, went to shows, and partied together.

Each day was a different experience. Of all the islands, Corfu, Mykonos, Olympia, and Santorini, Santorini was the best! The ship anchored in the Mediterranean Sea. There was a boat that got groups of us at a time and transported us to the Santorini Island. Once on the island, there were only 3 ways up the mountain to town. Cable car, donkey trail (we would be walking through donkey defecation), or Donkey ride. We heard the wait for the cable car was 2 1/2 hours so clearly we took the Donkey ride.

Choosing the donkey ride was the most amazing experience I had. There were about 100 donkeys and each donkey carried 1 person at a time, up this beautiful White Mountain while admiring this sky blue sea, the higher up we got the more amazing the view became. The donkey carried us up this circular mountain which had a rail that was about 3 feet high, so the donkey was taller than the rail. What made this experience the highlight was my fear of heights. This donkey had to have sensed my fear because he kept walking so close to the edge of the mountain while shaking his head over the ledge.

So between getting higher in the mountain, looking at the ship becoming smaller and the businesses and homes embedded in the mountain was just simply satisfying. Our Colombian friend was on the donkey in front of us. His donkey snapped and turned around and began heading downwards galloping at a good speed. As my friend flew past I was so afraid for him and secretly for myself hoping my donkey wouldn't follow his. He also was afraid. His eyes were bucked and he had the rope so tight and his back was stiff, for he sat up so straight trying to keep his balance from the speed. Suddenly a Greek man spoke loud to the donkey and the donkey stopped, turned around and began walking up the mountain again.

The donkey ride was the highlight of the Santorini experience. I learned later that the reason the homes and architecture is so white is because they have a substance that they cover the buildings with to keep rodents from entering. I wondered just how those buildings stayed so white. We made our own excursion so we started out getting mopeds. We visited Fira and Oia; we walked the island to see how the natives lived, and to the winery and enjoyed a wine tasting, then to the red beach. We went down a mountain to get to the beach where we took wonderful pictures.

Another island I'll always remember is Mykonos. Our Columbian friends accompanied us on another self-made excursion. We decided to rent a 4x4 drop top Suzuki for $50 dollars for the day including insurance. Today our Columbian friend drove so we could take pictures and journal. I didn't want to forget a thing! Two minutes into the excursion a Chinese woman driving an ATV four wheeler in front of us begins accelerating making a left turn onto oncoming traffic. We swerved to avoid hitting her but we collided anyway. The impact forced her from the ATV making her land on the ground. We were on a mountain incline, so naturally the jeep is rolling backwards but she was lying alongside the jeep so our friend had to hurry and extract the emergency brake. "She's not moving"!

The Greek pedestrians were spectating, calls were made to the police, and meanwhile my friend who is a nurse began assessing the injured woman. All of a sudden I see five ATV's riding towards us, it is the Chinese lady's group. They noticed she was no longer behind them so they turned around to seek her. Of all the people walking towards us I notice this tall Chinese guy wearing a black t-shirt with white lettering saying "Smile still alive"!

Wow, I thought to myself although this lady is laid out on the ground that has taken the skin from her body as a price to be paid for being on the ground, I couldn't help but shout and praise God in my spirit. For her friend to choose that shirt on the day an accident like this happens, that was nothing more than confirmation for me if not anyone else. I'm in Greece, after sacrificing and worry from all the obstacles that I have faced these past two years. "Smile still alive" and exploring Europe on a fixed budget. I was grateful because what was meant to be a negative instance turned around to be God's grace.

As I glanced at the woman whom stood up with help, and the vehicle we drove that now had an upside down frown front end, her ATV that had no driver turn light and the ferine that had fallen to the ground, and the 4x4 had a big dent above the front passenger tire, I could only say, "Thank You Father". The police finished up the questioning and ruled us innocent. We were able to go back to the rental office and get another 4x4 to continue with our excursion. As we drove off, we were all smiling because we were still alive, in spite of whatever each of us faced in our personal lives.

We explored Mykonos. We ate a gyro and sat under a tree that was 205 years old. We had made plans to meet our friends from Dominican Republic at Paradise Beach so we headed there to end our day in Mykonos. Once we found our friends we all got lounge chairs and took pictures and played in the clear blue sea. We splashed water on one another and had interesting conversations about everything, we didn't know at first this was a nude beach till this pregnant woman walks past in her birthday suit, so I joined topless as well. We all tanned, I journaled and even took a nap. As it was time to leave, we all piled into the 4x4 jeep lapped up and headed back to the rental shop across the island. We laughed so hard while recording our adventure together.

My third eye was well appreciated on this vacation. In the beginning I questioned what would become of this cruise. After this day's journey I asked my inner self what was each person's purpose in our lives. Before long everything was revealed. My friend from Dominican Republic wrote her name and number along with a bible verse Job 42:14. I didn't question but I did say "I'm going to look this up", she said "I want you to"! Although we both were clueless for she was working in the spirit when she first spoke and invited me to sit with her and her close friend. It wasn't till I returned home, got the bible and turned to Job 42.

I went to verse 14 and I decided to start at verse 1, the beginning, what did it say but…. Job is restored! I thought praise God, Katerria is restored! I survived from the manner that God gave me throughout this experience and it was sufficient. I purchased a beautiful kitchen mat that lies under the kitchen sink. This mat is a portrait of a Venice apartment front I got a year ago. As I stood in the kitchen washing dishes, I looked down under my feet and smiled "Wow…I've been there"!

A Six Pack & Some Curly Fries
By: Brenda L. Stovall

This is a true story. They names have been
changed but the logic is just the same of how we as
women let others use us and don't value our net worth.
It was a fall day and I was at my girl's house when two
of her friends, Shaba Doo and Romell came through for
a card game. We all joked how Romell thought he was
Montel Williams and he did have striking features
resembling the talk show mogul down to his caramel
colored skin and shiny bald head, but his side kick, was
something else to be reckoned with...a total
resemblance of Napoleon Dynamite's brother from size,
stature, and appearance from his stringy, greasy hair
waving to me in different directions, skin resembling a
glass of ice cold milk, nerdy, shy, and on the milk carton
for missing trailer park hopeful.

As the hands were being dealt Romell proceeded
to tell us about Shaba Doo who we just found out spent
time in the military (in who's army so I thought as I
peeped my hand) and his latest date with a Brazilian
Beauty! (Be mindful this is the early 90's where
beepers and pay-per-view fight parties were the big
thing) Next thing I knew Romell's animated body
springs up from the table as he can't stand still (or play
cards for that matter, therefore holding up the game)
as he starts to tell us about his matchmaking to fix

173

Shaba Doo up with a friend of his named Lourdes who had been separated for a while and wanted Shaba Doo to take her out to dinner for a nice time because she was new in town and just to have some company...that's it!!!

Now the story started getting good because Romell began to tell us how cheap Shaba Doo was (we could tell by his clothes and appearance combined with his military rationed eyewear). "Yeah I asked Shaba Doo to take Lourdes out and he says 'I don't have no money to take her out'!" as I stepped into the kitchen to get a sip of Malibu Rum and Coke as the smell of my girlfriend's Virginia Slims filled the air.

I left my Newports at home and took a puff of one of her cancer sticks which tasted like air to my normal drag and wasn't worth the hit I was used too as I got comfortable on the couch because our card game was about over all due to Romell's theatrics as his eyes were opened wide with his cards sprayed in his hand so no one would look as he commenced telling us the chain of events:

"This chick's body was banging, small waist, cute in the face, petite and gorgeous hair and an accent out of this world. I introduced them and since Shaba Doo never had any money, and I wanted this girl to have a nice time with dinner, movie, and a night on the town, I cancelled my Pay-Per-View Mike Tyson Fight and gave the money to Shaba Doo to take Lourdes out to have a good time! Shaba Doo tells me that he 'never spends that kind of money for a date' and I told him that's why he doesn't have a woman and a classy one like this! So, they go out for the night on the date and I'm so ashamed and disgusted! Shaba Doo, _YOU_ tell you the rest of the story!"

Shabo Doo with his Napoleon Dynamite's Brother "look-a-like self" proceeded to tell us the chain of events for the night..."Yeah, I told Romell that I never spent that type of money on a chick before so I go picked her up in my Chevy Nova and she was banging as Romell said. So I ask her did she want something to eat and she said "yeah" so we went to 7-11 and got us some beers and then went to the drive through at Checkers and got us some curly fries and we went back to my place and she gave it up for a 6 pack and some curly fries! I told Romell he's a fool for spending all that type of money for a chick and she gave it up to me on the first night, for some curly fries...!"

Then Romell chimes in..."Can you believe she gave it up to Shaba Doo and all he spent on her was some cash for a 6 pack and some curly fries! I cancelled my pay-per-view fight for her and here it is Shaba Doo has a pocket full of cash to spend on her and she gives it up for a 6 pack and some curly fries! Why do you women do that! I could have kept my money! And then I miss the fight! Didn't she know she was worth more than that! All I wanted him to do is take her out to dinner and have a nice time, not to sleep with my boy! And she's a married woman??? What's up with that!"

175

I sat there stunned and thought about how we as women give it up for less than that and men won't even open doors or call you by your name, but you will allow someone to take the most intimate part you have to offer it for less than that! Here it is this Brazilian beauty didn't know her worth and she was gorgeous because she came to my 27th Birthday Party with Shaba Doo a few months later.

The whole room was astonished by her beauty and couldn't believe she would even date this moron let alone sleep with him! And here it is 15 years later and those words are still etched in my mind as I've been celibate for 13 plus years by choice because I know my worth and will not give it up for a 6 pack and some curly fries let alone for free!

Question is...how much did he pay to get yours?

Just Another Day At The Office
By: Linda D. Gaddis

Carolina Samantha Neely Price. That was her name and she was proud of it. That is why she repeated it over and over again as she revisited her reflection in the distance. Her reflection was found in a small pool of water only a few feet away from her. It was slightly pass five in the morning as she began to prepare for her day. Getting up at and before the crack of dawn was something she had gotten used to. She had been schooled early, that in order to get ahead in life, you had to get up early. And so she did.

The early morning skies were still dark as she began to gather her clothes and perform her daily grooming rituals. "Cleanliness is next to Godliness", she recalled having her grandmother say, as she combed her fingers through the massive formation of curls that engulfed her face. She gave herself a few extra counts as she brushed her teeth. Fifty-seven Mississippi, Fifty-eight Mississippi, Fifty-nine Mississippi, Sixty! Ah, clean she thought to herself as she rolled her tongue over the smooth surface of her front teeth.

She remembered her mother saying, "The

longer you brush the better job you do on eliminating the germs that cause your teeth to decay giving you cleaner teeth, a brighter smile and a fresher breath". Carolina chuckled to herself every time she thought about her mother saying that. It always sounded like a commercial for some toothpaste or mouthwash. As she continued to ready herself, she pondered that thought further. Maybe it wasn't her mother, maybe it was her teacher that had had given her that advice.

It really didn't matter who said it, it was pretty sound advice and Carolina embraced it. Pulling up her stockings, she put the final touches on her wardrobe. Everything had to be just so in order for that "layered look" to be effective. She had chosen her shoes carefully, because there would be plenty of walking in store for her today. She was now ready to step off the curb and onto the streets.

Carolina was a salesperson. She had the "patience of Job" and the wisdom of a scholar. People weren't always kind to her, nor did they have kind things to say to her. But, this didn't stop her from doing her j-o-b. Her 'feathers' were never 'ruffled'. And she would never allow her 'knickers' to get into 'a bunch'. Outgoing and optimistic, Carolina approached each day. Never allowing "naysayers" to keep her down, her co-workers, although not always displaying the same disposition, were very supportive. If she had forgotten her lunch, they would all pitch in and "help a sister out". They would make sure she had something to eat. She would do the same for them.

The people in the corner building where she reported daily were always happy to see her and greeted her the same way each time. The day would always seem to go faster when everyone worked together. There weren't that many employees at her site. But, all the faithful who showed up every morning were grateful for the opportunity to work and gave it their all. Their customer service skills were exemplary and those who
couldn't "cut the mustard", were encouraged to seek employment elsewhere.

Many of the workers were now beginning to feel the stress of the day as the sun made its pilgrimage west. Others were so caught up in their endeavors; they had forgotten to take lunch. It was plain to see at this point, that all parties involved were tired and were willing to call it a day. Carolina ended her day with a cheery goodbye and a "see you later" along with the statement she would make to those she would greet throughout the day..."God bless you."

Going back always required more energy than coming out. Her feet were swollen from the constant travel to and fro and being on them all day. Her legs ached as well. Her throat was raw from the constant verbal exchange. Her lips were parched due to the excessive heat throughout the day.

As Carolina walked ever so slowly down the street she thought about her day. She thought about how grateful she was to be alive and to have made another day on the job. Marcy and Telly Mann weren't so lucky. Marcy was run over by a sixteen wheeler as she crossed the street last weekend.

Telly Mann didn't fare that much better. Monday, up around 9th street, he was viciously attacked by a group of about ten undisciplined youth. They took a metal bat and beat him 'til he could no longer move and his head burst open like an over ripened melon exposing his brains which spilled out onto the concrete. His last words as he underwent this ordeal were "have mercy, please, have mercy. His attackers showed no mercy or compassion as they walked away with a well-worn Bulls cap, a pair of Nike 'knock offs' and $2.17 he had accumulated over the course of two weeks from his socks,

As Carolina rounded the corner and approached the overhead pass, she stepped up onto the curb where she entered a space she called home. It was dark now, and the night couldn't have come too soon. In a few hours she would be up and at it again. But for now, she would take a moment to relax. Tonight was Wednesday and the Sox played a home game, so that meant entertainment and fireworks.

If she hurried, she could do her laundry during the sixth inning. She would use the water she had collected in the large metal 'hominy corn' can she had found in the streets that Sunday and the soap she had acquired from the nearby gas station on her way home. She diligently scrubbed the items she would be wearing the next day and hung them up to dry on the fence that served as a wall behind her.

She then rustled through a Jewels ' shopping cart that served as a storage case for all of her prized possessions. She shuffled through her belongings until she located her make shift pillow, made from an old discarded flannel shirt stuffed with crumbled newspaper, and a moth riddled blanket that had blown out of the window of a badly wrecked car about a year ago. This Carolina would use to fend off the wicked winter winds that could prove unbearable during the long and often unrelenting months ahead in "the Windy".

As she pulled out the cardboard castle that was lodged behind the metal shopping cart she began to settle in for the night. Carolina looked up at the sky and wished upon the one lone star playing 'hide-n-seek' behind one lone cloud lingering from earlier in the day. She sang her song to the tune of "Silent Night": "Silent Night, homeless night. All is calm. Save my life." This she did as she knelled alongside her cardboard bed with her make shift pillow and discarded blanket and prayed.

Stretching out now and looking once again towards the heavens she witnessed another home run as celebrated by the fireworks lighting up the skies over the park. Occasionally, brushing away the tears that welled up in her eyes as she briefly, ever so briefly reflected upon her past and reminisced about what would've been, until the game ended and she fell, with a smile, off to sleep.

Fire Ball of Confusion
By: Adrienne Bruce

One Saturday afternoon while I was standing in the long checkout line browsing through the tabloids, a short, stout senior citizen whom reminded me of Aunt Bee on the Andy Griffin show pushed her cart next to mine.

"May I go before you I only have two items?"

"Sure go ahead."

"Aunt Bee" I said to myself, while she walked past me leaving a scent of lilac blossoms in the air. In her cart were two paintings. I could only see one of the paintings. It was a large painting of two women; one with a lamp shape of a hat on top of her head and the other woman's hands appeared to be glued to a crystal ball. She looked so strange! I could almost hear her soft raspy voice.

"Elizabeth there seems to be a deep dark family secret that has been lurking around for at least forty years."

The room grew darker and the smoke filled sphere lit the entire room as the fortune teller's wide eyes gazed into it. In a wicked voice she states, "Your grandfather Lewis owned a cotton plantation and has purchased several slaves right off the auction block to tend to the fields"

"How did you know?"

As the fortune teller's bony hand waved over the ball, she took a deep breath and stated,

"You inherited a lot of money didn't you?"

The tassels on Elizabeth's hat began to vibrate as she shook in fear.

"No one knows about that money, who told you?" The frail lady laughed

"Yeah, I'm the fortune teller but you are the fortune owner. Grandpa Lewis was an evil man. For three years straight his cotton plantation suffered a drought which financially drained him. One night Old Man Louie couldn't rest because the banker threatened to foreclose on his property and he was desperate. He couldn't handle the pressure so he went out to the old shed and grabbed a gasoline can."
"Stop!
Yelled Elizabeth;
I don't want to hear anymore"

She stood up and began to cry as the feeble old Fortune Teller says;

"Oh no…You're going to get your money's worth! You paid for one hour and you have fifteen minutes left! You need to know the truth! Sit down!!!"

The fortune teller pointed her fingers as Elizabeth plopped down in the high back, red velvety chair as she took out a handkerchief to wipe her eyes.
"OK! Just what did Uncle Louie do?
The old fortuneteller eyes rolled back in her head like two white marbles never to return.
"Are you ready for the truth honey?"
"What! What did he do?

She clasped her hanky real tight to her chest.

"Ole Louie took the gas can and spread gasoline around the house on the plantation as if he were watering the grass. All the slaves were still sleeping in the servant quarters. There were two large families that had served Louie for years. Oh, how Louie loved his Cuban cigars! He took out a match and lit the cigar and tosses the match onto the gas soaked grass"

Elizabeth started screaming and the crystal ball burst into flames. The old fortuneteller slumped back in her chair.

"Excuse me Miss! Miss! Will that be a check or cash?"
"Oh, I'm sorry, you caught me daydreaming!"
I took my wallet out.
"That will be cash..."

A New Day
By: Kelly Clark

I felt her looking down on me with disdain and disapproval. I know she was thinking, "How on Earth did we both get here?" She was shocked! She was enraged! I knew she just wanted to kick me and all my caramel assets all over the office! She knew, however, if she did, that would be the last straw! All of her dignity, her grace and her beauty would be lost.

So, instead, she just hovered; right over me. Those seconds felt like hours. I could feel her eyes burning into me. Her breath violently blowing in my face! I could see her physically trembling. I knew if I made the slightest move at that moment, she would completely snap!

After all, she had lost everything and all she had "was "this moment! She needed to be graceful and dignified and I was graceful and dignified enough to give her "the moment". I had nothing to lose by submitting to her so I did. It was actually at that moment that I came to understand what the bible meant when it said that beauty was passing. For, it was at that moment, when her beauty had passed and mine had just begun...

You see, our story didn't begin here. It began several years back. I had just started my new job and she was the boss's wife. And yes, she was beautiful. She had a presence about her that made not just the men turn their heads but the women too! She was tall and shapely and always dressed in the latest fashions with the greatest price tags. Her jewels were one-of-a-kind and here fragrance was top of the line.

Then, her shoes, can I tell you about her shoes! I mean, her shoes were so tough; they put her clothes, fragrance, purses and hair to shame! Really! They were cold, hot, high and sharp...and so was she! Everybody knew it too. She ran her husband's company like a mesmerizing mogul. She held the meetings, she called the shots, and she did the hiring and firing. It was like the boss turned everything over to her! We never really saw the boss, actually. We would just get his monthly memos, evaluations, state of the company addresses and holiday greetings. Everything else came from her.

Folks said she even ran the company while she was pregnant with all three of her children! It's like she never missed a beat. The job profited from it too! The company's shares doubled three times, in the last ten years! She had a charm and finesse that attracted the top talents from around the world. Both China and Japan reached out to her for the training of their associates because she was just that good! Yes, she was woman who had really done well for herself!

Then there was me. I remember praying for a good job, anywhere, at any company! I had grown weary of being at jobs with unscrupulous managers and bosses that wasted and misuse company resources. Then, when the company is in crisis, they encumber working conditions, pilfer pensions and castigate employees. They blame the employees, their benefits and their salaries for all the setbacks and layoffs. Now, when the crisis gets too great, the big bosses resign with all the company's money in Swiss Bank Accounts, with their names on them.

Meanwhile, the staunch employees are left with

nothing for all of their labor. The CEO's and managers seem to never pay for their misdeeds. It wasn't fair and I wanted to be somewhere that would be different. I wanted to be free to work and enjoy the fruits of my labor. I wanted to feel safe at my job and be fulfilled. Then, a friend told me that there was a company that was hiring. They had a great starting salary, opportunity for growth and the benefits where great.

I looked into it and applied. I prayed that if God would give me this job, I would work hard and go the extra mile. I would pay my tithes and my offerings and I would invest in others. I promised not to steal company pens or any other office supplies. I would not try to leave the office before time or get friends to punch me in if I was running late. I really wanted the job and "praise the Lord"...I got it!

I worked hard too. I did overtime and weekends when they asked. I worked with charitable organizations within the company and without. I didn't steal substance or time. I gave to others and helped out whenever I could. I prayed for the owners of the company and all the upper and middle management. I was happy, and I was in a good place in my life.
Then something happened!

I walked into my office as I had done on many years of Mondays before. I got to the office around 8:15am with laptop and three Krueg pods in hand; Cafe Escapes, Chai Latte; Emeril's "Big Easy Bold and Green Mountains, Caramel Vanilla Cream. These were my "must haves" to get me through the day. I walked over to my copiously spaced cubicle. I put down my laptop and started my Chai Tea in the Krueg, as I made my way to the restroom, to relieve my bladder and revive my makeup.

When I returned, I grabbed my favorite Wonder Woman cup and sipped on my latte as I plopped into my ergonomic and comfy chair. This was why I arrived early. I could take the time to relax and meditate before I started my working day. I had a great view of the park with the pond, where the swans would always offer pleasurable moments of interest and reflection.

Just as I said my last prayer and sipped my last sip of tea, my eyes were drawn to a surprisingly healthy and fit form positioned in the opening of my cubicle. I felt my heart skip a beat as my eyes moved from the Ferragamo shoes, to the Caraceni suit up to a vaguely familiar chiseled face I've only seen once before.

As I breathed in, my latte aroma gave way to the sublime effluvium of fragrance coming from his direction. As I exhaled, my brain caught up to the reality of who this was present with me, here, in my cubicle! I began to think, "How could this be?'

My mind began to explode with questions, but nothing came out of my mouth; no matter how hard I tried. I noticed how my heart was beating so fast, I thought it would burst right out of my chest. Then I remembered to breathe in, and then out, in, then out. Now calm and ready, I began to open my mouth to speak, when he spoke instead. His voice had a way of rendering you helpless and commanding your undivided attention.

"Hello." He said.
"I can't believe I'm finally able to meet the beautiful woman that saved my life."

He announced, as he clapped both his hands gently together.

"How is this possible?" I shrieked!

"You never met me or knew where I lived, let alone worked!"

"Money has a way of answering many questions." He responded.

You see, this man was born with a silver spoon in his mouth. He was an aristocratic philanderer. He had the best of everything. He didn't know what generic brands were until he was well into his adult years. He went to the best of schools and had the best of circumstance. He was traveled and well versed in many languages. Women were at his beck and call. He lived a very liberated and care free life. But, when his family decided it was time for him to settle down, they chose from only the most beautiful of women who were raised in the most exclusive families. His wife was from the best of schools and social forums. She lived a very privileged and diaphanous life as well.

They're union brought the respect and admiration of many. Their wealth and power multiplied. But one day, in the apex of their reign, the man got sick. He got very sick and remained that way for many years. This changed his devil may care attitude to that of reflection, regret and repentance. This also changed his wife's demeanor. She began to organize calamitous enterprises against him. After all, she wanted what was rightfully due her. She would rather see him dead, than alive and weak. She had accomplished a lot and stood to gain even more.

The man's sickness turned fatal. He needed a blood transfusion but had a very rare blood type. When his children were called forth to offer blood, to the families apocalypse, they were not compatible. Everyone thought for sure the man would die. Then a trusted friend from his youth suggested that his parents reach out to the sperm bank that many of his collegiate, including this man, donated to as part of their fraternal inductions. With success, the parents discovered his specimen was used to source one child.

The parents continued to work with the agency to reach the mother and inform her of the donor's predicament. They asked if she would bring the child, all expenses paid, to this exclusive hospital to give blood? Not knowing what to expect, she prayed about it, then conceded. She only saw the donor once. He was unconscious. She prayed for his health and recovery, and then her and her son returned home. When the man recovered he inquired at the agency to get the whereabouts of the mother and son who saved his life. Because the man was very wealthy, the agency gave him everything he needed to know.

"It surprised me when I discovered that you worked at one of my companies." He said.

"Your company?" I gasped!

"You mean, this is your company and that's your wife who's been running things?" I asked.

"Yes and No" He said.

"Yes. This is my company and No. That was my wife, who uses to run things!"

"That's the second reason I'm here." He announced.

"I'm here to see that my ex-wife removes all her belongings and leaves my company! She has been very corrupt in her business dealings and with me. She has been in partnership with a rival of mine to take the company from me. She has been unfaithful in our marriage and deceptive of our children. She has hurt me very deeply. I wanted to hate her and retaliate, but I have learned to forgive."

"So" He said sadly,

"I am here to end one era of my life and begin another. I want to purge my company and start anew and I want to get to know my ten year old son and his mother, if you let me?"

It was at this time that the bosses ex-wife came out of her office, box in hand. By the look on her face, she had been briefed on who I was and what me and my son had done. She was not pleased. If he had died, everything would be hers. No one would be the wiser. Who would ever imagine something like this? Focused however, she walked straight toward us, glanced atrociously at him, then stopped at me; and this, is where our story began.

When her moment had expired, I graciously stepped out of her way and watched as she fumed out of the office, out of the building and out of our lives forever.

.....Dont get it twisted!

Charm is deceitful and beauty is passing,
But a woman who fears the Lord, she shall be praised.
Give her of the fruit of her hands
And let her own works praise her in the gates.

Proverbs 31:30-31(NKJ)

Biographies

Adrienne Bruce

Adrienne Bruce established the P.O.P (Pen on Paper) writer's guild for the purpose of amassing individuals who are like-minded and have a passion for expressing themselves through a variety of writing styles.

POP provides a creative space for gifted writers to indulge in new ideas and share their inner thoughts and feelings through an array of publications.

Bruce freely gives credit where credit is due, recognizing that she inherited her parents' artistic overflow. Bruce's talent and appreciation for the arts, spans across many generations of her family. Her father, once a window designer for several State Street department stores, also painted murals in Chicago's Hyde Park neighborhood; while her mother passed down her artistic talents through teaching Adrienne how to loom, crochet, sew and cook.

A native Chicagoan, Adrienne Bruce is also a former Cosmetology Teacher with the Chicago Public School. She invested many years teaching in an industry that promotes education, fashion and design.

Whether styling hair, painting a landscape, designing a piece of jewelry or writing poetry, creating beauty is what's most intriguing to her

Mrs. Adrienne Bruce believes that "Creating with your hands dates back to the beginning of time. God created the heavens and the earth. He formed and fashioned life through the creation of Man. Each of us are blessed with a God given ability to create in our own individual and unique way. Many People today are not utilizing their natural God-given talents, or even trying to discover their inner gifts. Throughout history our cultural customs have served as a storehouse of our innate talents and abilities. I believe that our historical customs should be retrieved, embraced and regenerated for future generations".

 *Brenda L. Stovall*

Brenda L. Stovall is the founder of The Writing Is On The Wall Poetry, Publication & Productions, NFP (WOTW, NFP) and the Executive Producer & Host of the He...Brews! Radio Broadcast which airs on Chicago's Big Gospel Express WBGX AM1570 which has been in existence since 2005. She's interviewed numerous guests including *TLN's Aspiring Women's* former Co-Host, and Author, Michelle McKinney Hammond.

W.O.T.W., NFP is a nonprofit organization whose purpose is to utilize the Literary, Creative/Graphic, & Performance Arts as a tool to empower, motivate, minister, & educate individuals into making morally sound decisions. They've partnered with various organizations including Sarah's Inn, The Jason Foundation, Advocate Healthcare, and Mercy Hospital creating awareness of Domestic Violence, Teen Suicide, Abstinence, and Self-Mutilation.

She holds an Associate's Degree in Paralegal Studies from MacCormac College, a Bachelor's Degree in Business Administration with a concentration in Project Management from Colorado Technical University, and currently a Graduate Student at Argosy University majoring in I/O Psychology.

Ms. Stovall has studied under Actor/Author & Instructor John Starrs at DePaul University for Poetry & Theater as well as renowned poet, Geoffrey "Dr. Groove" Watts, and has worked in Drama Ministry for various organizations including; Life Christian Center International of Bellwood, IL, Holy Nations Ministry of Naperville, IL., and with DePaul University's Divine Living Word Campus Ministry by writing and directing the play, *"Slapping Domestic Violence Back In The Face"* which was performed at DePaul's Lincoln Park Student Center for two shows November 2004 and brought back by popular demand at the *Merle Reskin Theater* of Chicago for a charity fundraiser to build a homeless shelter for victims of domestic violence January 2005.

Her other theatrical productions include; *"Sex Money & Communication"*, *"Fashion in the Church"*, *"The Lord & Tailor"*, *"7 Brides, But There's Only Just 1 Brother"*, and appeared as an actress for Jkbu Productions Inc. & The Chicago Playwright Fellowship production of the Gospel Comedy Stage Play, "The Church Program Is Subject To Change" as Evangelist Tabitha and several radio & television appearances for poetry performances including CAN-TV's the "Tocorra Rodgers' Show", "Hearts of Praise", "Thread the Needle", "The Effie Roth Show", & a culinary critic for "Check Please!" and featured in the July 2006 issue of Pioneer Press.

She also worked with New Beginning Productions, LLC., writing and directing the internet series, "Take This

Job &...", and is the author of "*Forget Reach & Press...a poetical approach to my recovery & discovery*" with Author House Publishing and now currently working on her next project, "*Renaissance, The Rebirth & Revision of the Black Man and Woman*" also with Author House Publications and served on "The Voice" Newsletter for Broadview Baptist Church & assisted their Project Management Team with an article on Change to assist with logistics moving into a larger facility,

Ms. Stovall is available for writing/directing, seminars, workshops and speaking engagements.

Phone: (708) 505-WOTW (9689)
Email: info@thewritingisonthewall.org
Web: www.thewritingisonthewall.org
Facebook: The Writing Is On The Wall Poetry
Publications & Productions, NFP

 Katerria "Starr" Doty

Katerria "Starr" Doty was born in Chicago 1977 where she currently resides. She graduated from Olive Harvey with her Associates in Early Childhood Education. She works at her home daycare which she founded 2004.

Katerria is the happy mother of two daughters, Timerria and Winter Starr Daniel. Katerria loves her family and friends, nature and being outdoors, animals, reading, entertaining, poetry, children, live music, and of course traveling.

Katerria is grateful to almighty God for all she's seen and experienced thus far, and is looking forward to what
lies ahead.

Linda Diane Gaddis

Linda Diane Gaddis was born in Chicago, Illinois, but lived at times in Denver, Colorado and Cleveland, Ohio. During her adolescent years, she would travel down south and spend most of every summer on her great grandmother's farm. It was here she gained an appreciation for family and a respect for nature.

Linda grew up on the south side of Chicago. She attended grade school at Charles S. Deneen, where she acquired her appreciation of books and the fine arts. Her high school years were among her happiest. Robert Lindblom Technical High School is where she learned drafting and participated in an array of sports.

Linda loved teaching. She began her teaching profession on the west side, at Emmett North and the south side at Walter H. Dyett Middle School. It was at Dyett she thrived under the mentorship of Dr. Yvonne Minor. She taught reading and science. She worked with the Chicago Public Schools science department and the Science Fairs on the regional, city and state levels. She was spotlighted in a film presentation on *Teaching Reading Through Drama* and also in a video used by the Board of Education to promote the use of cooperative learning in the classroom. Her and her students were featured in a documentary produced by

WTTW, *"About the Children"*. It was also during her stay at Dyett that she met the legendary Bill Kurtis and worked with a group of teachers to help write curriculum and promote his series, *"The New* Explorers *Program"*.

Linda has worked with the ETA Theater in Chicago where she starred in a summer production at Chicago State University and appeared as an extra in the movies *"Barber Shop II"* and *"Roll Bounce"*.

Linda enjoys being a member of "Sistah's", a group of African American women who come together once each month to communicate with, about and for the arts as they celebrate life and have a good time. And yes, she has a bucket list. Now that she has retired, she plans to take up several hobbies. They include writing, photography, acting, art, sewing, crafts, studying another language, and learning how to 'step'. She plans to travel, revisiting Ghana and Kenya, and other remote and exotic parts of the world. Her biggest adventure is to take a road trip visiting all fifty states in the U.S.

Linda is currently self-publishing a book of poetry entitled, *"First Fruits"*, *to* be released in August, 2012. She will use some of the proceeds from the sale of her books to start a non-profit organization and establish educational and literary programs for both children and adults.

You can contact Linda on-line at:
www.lgpapertrail1@gmail.com
www.FirstFruitsSite.com

JoAnn Wesley Hassler

What if you could achieve life balance, enhance your relationships and deepen your faith in just a few minutes each day? Research has proved journal writing is a valuable tool in handling life circumstances from chronic illness to time-management. The challenge is finding the time to access the value. Let JoAnn Wesley Hassler show you how to use this valuable resource in a time efficient and effective manner. Discover your voice and wisdom five minutes at a time.

JoAnn Wesley Hassler is passionate about journal writing. She has been recording her own words, thoughts and feelings consistently for the past twenty five years. As a spiritual director and professional coach, she encourages her clients to find their voice and through the written word. She believes there is a writer's voice within each of us that is pleading to be heard. All that voice needs is the right powerful question, prompt or encouragement, just a bit of time and attention to allow the muse to step forth. She firmly upholds the benefits of journal writing for personal development, spiritual growth and professional intensification.

JoAnn received her Bachelor of Arts Degree in 2009 from DePaul University in Chicago, Illinois in which her focus area was Training, Mentoring and Spiritual Direction. She holds a Certification in Spiritual Direction from the Haden Institute in North Carolina, a coaching certification from Coach Training Alliance and a certification in Journal Writing from the Center for Journal Therapy in Lakewood, Colorado.

As a coach, JoAnnHasslerCoaching: Self Coach to Success strategizes with Realtors and Entrepreneurs on time management and goal setting to create a balanced and prosperous life. She has been coaching Re/Max Realtors since 2004. As a Realtor and Independent Contractor for over twenty years, she knows the challenges and the great joys of creating and sustaining a business in all economic climates. As a Trainer, Corporate Coach and Manager she coaches, consults and companions business professionals on their journey.

JoAnn is the author and presenter of _Self Coach to Success for Real Estate Professionals_ and is writing a book on the use of journal writing for professional development and problem solving. She currently serves on the Advisory Board for Benedictine University's Center for Lifelong Learning and is an instructor in the program.

She is a sought after speaker and offers programs on Goal Setting and Time Management, The Toolbox for Self Coaching and the use of Journal Writing for personal development, spiritual enhancement and professional clarity.

As a spiritual director, she offers classes and retreats on journal writing, dream work, vision boards and creative collage. JoAnn believes a life well lived is a balanced life filled with satisfying work, fulfilling relationships and time to reflect on all the pieces of the puzzle we call life.

Ken Allison

How can one define the true Power and Soul of Mr. Ken Allison? The Power of Mr. Ken Allison is the intensity in which he approaches the music. Whether it is during a live performance or in a studio session, it is a relationship that only God, Ken, and the music can understand. The Soul of Mr. Ken Allison can be defined as quintessential.

He is an exemplary entertainer whose career spans over four decades. This dedication alone is evident he indeed has soul. While on stage, he believes that it is his soul responsibility to entertain the least impressionable and rigid of nonbelievers. His performance is captivating and pure magic.

The power of his performance is something that one must experience to fully appreciate. By the end of every performance, everyone will attest to the Power and Soul of Mr. Ken Allison. Ken Allison was personally trained by Bobby Miller (writer/arranger/producer of the Mighty Mighty Dells of Chicago, Illinois).

In the course of his career, Ken has opened for some of the biggest names in entertainment; Gladys Knight, David Ruffin, T-Connection, Billy Eckstine, The Miracles, Marlena Shaw, to name a few; and is called a friend by many others.

If the old adage, longevity has its rewards, is true then Ken Allison's career has earned him the reward of success. Ladies and Gentlemen... (As heard over the excitement of an enthusiastic crowd) ...prepare to experience the Power and Soul of the one and only Mr. Ken Allison.

Contact Ken Allison:
Phone: (773) 971-9318

 Kelly Clark

Kelly Clark was born and raised in Chicago Illinois. She attended the University of Illinois at Chicago and Chicago State University where she graduated with honors and received her Bachelors of Science degree.

Later she was accepted into the Star Teacher Program and received a scholarship to attend Concordia University where she graduated *Cum Laude with* a Masters in Curriculum and Instruction.

Kelly has been teaching in the Chicago Public School system for over 18 years. She began her career teaching 5th grade and went on to teach 7th grade, 7th-8th grade Departmental Social Studies, 3rd-5th Grade Honors and now teaches 1st grade.

Before her teaching career, Kelly worked in the State Pre-Kindergarten Program as a Social Worker Assistant where she collaborated with a facilitator, social worker, nurse and a team of teachers to help SPK Teachers, and parents find educational and community services needed to help them successfully transition their students into school. It was there where Kelly compiled and co-published a community directory used by over 22 area schools and their parents.

Kelly has always had a love for young people in and out of Chicago. She was a Program Director for 10 years at Circle Y Ranch a Christian camp in Bangor Michigan. She also served as its L.I.T. (Leaders-In-Training) Director for over 4 years where she trained teenagers ages 13-18 to serve in leadership positions at the camp and beyond.

Kelly went on to serve, first as a member of Circle Y Ranch Ladies' Auxiliary, and then as its President where they raised hundreds of thousands of dollars for the camp.

When Kelly is not teaching, she has enjoys a tutoring, designing jewelry, painting, and now writing. Currently, she is working on writing children's books that she can one day introduce to her classroom and many classrooms and homes around the globe.

Kelly can be reached at www.kellyclark1@ymail.com

 Lenita McCullor

My name is Lenita "FearlesSpeakz" McCullor. I was born and raised in Chicago. I'm a mother of two beautiful daughters, Shania who's 8 years old and Samaria who's 5 years old. I would like to start off by giving honor and glory to God who is the head of my life. I would like to thank my parents Clark and Sandra Hall for raising me to be the woman I am today and for their countless support and belief in me. I also want to thank my wonderful Great, Great Grandmother, Katie Mae Cooper, for her strength and her words of wisdom that's forever embedded within me.

In 6th grade, my English Teacher, Ms. White, told me that I was a good writer and that she enjoyed reading my story's (that were always due at the end of the week)! In my freshman year in high school, I fell in love with hip hop and its whole dynamic delivery of it. A few artists who inspired me to continue writing were; Talib Kweli, Mos Def, KRS-One, The Roots, Arrested Development and many more.

These artists are all poets in their own way, and so am I. Poetry to me is a relief. It can be your fix when you need a hit. It's a right path to eternal life if you deliver your message right. You have to love poetry because it's your thoughts, your style, and how you emotionally connect with your pieces that bring your message alive and every word can save somebody's life.

I've been employed with the University of Chicago Medical Center for 13 years in Environmental Services. In addition, I'm the current owner of Breathe Free Cleaning Services which utilizes and promotes green products in our daily operations. I'm also certified by the TEECH Foundation educating the community on becoming "green".

It is my goal to provide you with the necessary tools needed for you to create an atmosphere of purity. If you are interested in learning how your business/home can benefit from our services, please contact me via phone or email. I can assure you that the products used are not only environmentally safe but will improve the ozone, eliminate sick buildings and provide a healthier environment for you, your family, your employees and customers.

Breathe Free Cleaning Services
Phone: (773)440-3118
Email: YouCanBreatheFree@gmail.com

*.

 Valerie Winkfield

Valerie Winkfield is a native of Chicago and loves it. Valerie grew up on the southside, attended Park Manor elementary school and graduated from Hirsch High School. She went on to pursue her education by attending Fisk University in Nashville Tennessee. It was there that she discovered her love for arts and crafts. Valerie only raised two sons, but comes from a large family of 7 sisters and 3 brothers. She always found time to be creative whether it was sewing, drawing, or cutting paper collages.

Ms. Winkfield is currently a pharmaceutical technician at Northwestern Hospital and has been there for 38 years and is looking forward to retiring. Val loves to cruise to the tropical islands every chance she gets. Taking much needed vacations gives her inspiration when she is in a creative mode. Though her job keeps her busy, she finds time to design beautiful exquisitely framed greeting cards.

Theses card are on display at many outdoor festivals. People are amazed at the intricate details she puts into every greeting card. These cards are fabulous works of art. Valerie also indulges is other art forms such as hand tied blankets with matching pillows, novelty tissue boxes, fragrant creams, and soaps.

Ms. Winkfield was honored to illustrate this publication. She said, "Just think, at one time this was only a hobby, but now it's a business that I didn't see coming...Thank you POP Writers Guild for giving me the opportunity to share my paper passion with the world!"

To see used images in full color visit:

Facebook: Val's Paper Passion
Contact Ms. Winkfield via email
Valspaperpassion@yahoo.com

For Speaking Engagements Contact:
WWW.POPWRITERS.COM
(773) 442-2POP
(773) 442-2767

Eyes of Life
By: Adrienne Bruce

When the day breaks
And the eyes of life open
Seconds, minutes, and hours
Spent in a place
That will not be
Your final destiny
When the day breaks
And the eyes of life open
No more
Where will you be?
When the night falls
And the day breaks again